P9-DES-259

WHAT
ARE YOU
TRUSTING
GOD FOR?

PRACTICAL PRINCIPLES TO
MAXIMIZE YOUR KINGDOM IMPACT

GREGG HINZELMAN
FOREWORD BY DR. RICK REED

The principles that Gregg Hinzelman shares in this book have had a profound impact on my life and ministry, so I'm thrilled that these concepts are now being made available to a wider audience. Read this book, and be encouraged to trust God to do greater things through you!

Arvind Balaram
Lead Pastor, Delhi Bible Fellowship, Gurgaon, India

I have always been impressed by Gregg's desire to use his life to have a major impact in this world for Christ. Over the last twenty years I have watched him grow, mature, struggle, persevere, handle adversity and become a very effective leader. This book shares the principles that he has lived out over this time with authenticity, honesty and humility.

Paul Henderson
Former NHL Hockey Player,
1972 Team Canada Summit Series Hero

This book not only contains life-changing truth every Christian needs to hear, it's also written by the kind of leader every Christian needs to follow. Prepare to be challenged, stretched and blessed. May Gregg's book have the same impact on you as Gregg's life has had on me.

Ted Duncan
Senior Pastor, Hope Church Mississauga

For many years I have witnessed the passion of this man to impact the world. This book is a reminder that bearing fruit it is not an option! Throughout his journey, Gregg Hinzelman shows us in a very simple way how to cultivate a heart that is willing to trust God for the impossible.

Oliver Marin
Student-Led Movements Team Leader with
Cru Latin America and The Caribbean

Gregg Hinzelman has distilled his real experiences of trusting God for unbelievable impact into a guide that ignites passion. Be warned, this book will ignite your flickering longing into a fiery blaze to daily and forever change the world around you in Jesus' name!

Kevin Cuz
National Campus Director, Athletes
in Action, Canada

I really appreciate Gregg's insights on visioning a bigger impact for Christ. It has encouraged me to think beyond my day-to-day professional career, and align my focus to a much broader Kingdom vision.

David Au Yeung
Co-Founder, Managing Director
of Engineering at Flipp

What Are You Trusting God For? Practical Principles to Maximize Your Kingdom Impact

Copyright © 2019 by Gregg Hinzelman

ISBN: paperback 978-1-9990558-0-6 | ebook 978-1-9990558-1-3

All rights reserved. No portion of this book may be reproduced, stored in a retrieval system, or transmitted in any form or by any means—electronic, mechanical, photocopy, recording, scanning, or other—except for brief quotations in critical reviews or articles, without the prior written permission of the publisher.

Unless otherwise noted, Scripture quotations are taken from The Holy Bible, New International Version® NIV® Copyright © 1973 1978 1984 2011 by Biblica, Inc.™ Used by permission. All rights reserved worldwide.

Scripture quotations taken from the New American Standard Bible® (NASB), Copyright © 1960, 1962, 1963, 1968, 1971, 1972, 1973, 1975, 1977, 1995 by The Lockman Foundation Used by permission. www.Lockman.org

The ESV Global Study Bible®, ESV® Bible Copyright © 2012 by Crossway. All rights reserved.

The Holy Bible, English Standard Version® (ESV®) Copyright © 2001 by Crossway, a publishing ministry of Good News Publishers. All rights reserved.

ESV Text Edition: 2016

Illustrations by Bill Livingstone, Circus Strategic Communications Inc., Georgetown ON

Back cover photography by Jessica Hinzelman

Cover design & inside layout, typesetting and pre-press preparation by Bill Glasgow

Printed in Canada by DPI Graphics Group Inc., Mississauga ON

Contents

This book is dedicated to the many, many people who have invested in my walk with Jesus, my personal development, and my equipping for ministry. I have been blessed by you beyond what words can express. This book is an extension of your Kingdom impact in my life.

Foreword

When it comes to trusting God for more, most of us settle for less.

That's why Gregg Hinzelman wrote this book. Gregg writes to challenge us to trust God for more than we normally do. He calls us to believe God could use our lives to impact others in a way that echoes into eternity.

This book is about trusting God for big things. Not big things in the way the world normally measures them. It's not about trusting God for a big house, a big name or big bank account. It's about trusting God for big impact on big numbers of people. It's about kingdom impact.

Does that stir something inside you? It does for me!

But this book is not just inspirational, it's also practical. It doesn't just stay up in the clouds of big dreams, it gets down to earth. Gregg coaches us on how to take steps of faith in our everyday lives.

Gregg has spent the last thirty years trusting God for big things. He's had a front row seat to watch God work in some amazing ways. And he's learned that God can work through ordinary Christians to produce extraordinary kingdom impact.

After reading *What Are You Trusting God For?* and working through the reflection exercises in the final chapter, the words of Ephesians 3:20-21 kept ringing in my heart:

> Now to him who is able to do far more abundantly that all we ask or think according to the power at work within us, to him be glory in the church and in Christ Jesus, throughout all generations, forever and ever. Amen.

If you are ready to have your faith strengthened and stretched, keep reading!

Dr. Rick Reed
President, Heritage College and Seminary
February 2019

Introduction

I sat in the back of the bus in stunned silence, staring out the window at the masses of people.

I was completely overwhelmed.

I had just spent the afternoon with my youth pastor, Doug Nuenke, and a friend, visiting a densely populated slum area in the middle of Port-au-Prince, Haiti. Over 200,000 people were packed together into this area that covered about two square miles. I was told that families of between 8-12 people here shared homes that were about the same size as my bedroom. They took turns sleeping because there simply wasn't enough room for all to sleep at the same time.

As we walked along the narrow pathway between these homes, we tried to avoid stepping into the trickling stream that ran down the middle of our path. It was explained to me that this stream served as the people's drinking water, cleaning water, and sewage. An ever-present stench floated around us in this hot, dirty, impoverished community.

Less than two years earlier, I was interviewing for a church internship position. The interviewer asked me, "What is the purpose of your life?"

I enthusiastically replied, "I want to impact the world for Christ!"

"That's a pretty big goal," he said.

"I know. But that's what I want to do."

I was 18 years old, and I was naively idealistic. Impacting the world seemed like a pretty good goal. I loved Jesus, and wanted as many people to know him as possible. But now, in the back of this bus, that goal seemed utterly, absurdly, out of reach.

The reality of the immensity of our world began to sink in: "Here I am on an island of eight million people that a few years ago I didn't even know existed," I thought. "How could I ever think that I could have an impact on the world?" At that moment, my dream died. I needed to come up with a smaller, more realistic vision.

It's been over thirty years since that dream-crushing day. Since that time, God has taken me full circle. The purpose of my life today? I want to impact the world for Christ!

In the years following that trip to Haiti, I began to understand that this vision, while massive and seemingly impossible, was not wrong or even idealistic. In fact, it lines up perfectly with Jesus' vision for his Church. Jesus did not send his disciples to simply minister to a small group in a corner of Jerusalem. He sent them out to change the world.

The Bible provides us with tools and strategies to allow us to have an impact that is "exceeding, abundantly beyond all we can ask or imagine" (Ephesians 3:20 NASB 1977). We just need to trust what God says, and then step out in faith to apply them to our lives.

The simple, yet profound principles I will share in this book are borne out of the Word of God and out of my personal experience. In my 30+ years of ministry, I have seen men and women of all ages used by God to have an impact far greater than they would have ever dreamed. I have been amazed that God has allowed me to have a ministry that has touched the ends of the earth. And if you knew me, you would be amazed too! I am not a tremendously gifted speaker, writer, theologian or leader. But I serve an amazing God who wants to use me . . . and you . . . to help see our world changed for his glory.

Isaiah 49:6 says,

> It is too small a thing for you to be my servant to restore the tribes of Jacob and bring back those of Israel I have kept. I will also make you a light for the Gentiles, that my salvation may reach to the ends of the earth.

And in II Chronicles 16:9, we are told, "For the eyes of the Lord range throughout the whole earth to strengthen those whose hearts are fully committed to him."

The opportunity and command that Jesus has provided us is too massive for us to settle for small dreams and plans. I am convinced that God wants to use each of us to have a Kingdom impact that is far beyond what we are currently thinking, if we are willing to be used by him.

In the pages that follow, we will explore eight practical principles that will allow us to expand our Kingdom impact and potentially change the world:

1) Develop a God-sized vision
2) Allow God's Holy Spirit to empower your life and ministry
3) Pray specific and God-sized prayers
4) Live with an eternal perspective
5) Focus on "changing the trees" for greater societal impact
6) Develop a habit of expanding your faith
7) Focus on spiritual multiplication
8) Develop and maintain a global focus

Before we start, however, I want to add a few caveats. First, there are no formulas with God that guarantee ministry "success." Sometimes he uses ministry struggles to shape our character, and sometimes God's timing isn't what we want it to be. And while I believe that he has provided a blueprint for a significantly large impact, God in his providence may call you to a much smaller and intimate ministry. And that is great! Not everyone is called to impact large numbers of people.

Also, God rarely provides us with explosive results overnight. As I will address in the final chapter, a sizeable ministry impact happens generally over a lifetime of obedience. The stories that I will share in this book have occurred over my 30+ years of ministry, so don't be discouraged if you don't see immediate results.

Finally, we can become more usable over time, as we learn from our mistakes, deal with sin areas in our lives, and mature in our faith.

I don't know the vision that God has laid on your heart. But I believe that God is asking you to trust him for far more than you are currently thinking. I am certain that he is calling a generation of men and women who are trusting him for a God-sized impact. I pray that he uses the principles in this book to give you the spark you need to step out and be used by him in a world-changing way.

CHAPTER 1

What Are You Trusting God For?

In 1806, a group of students from Williams College in Williamstown, Massachusetts had been meeting twice weekly to pray for revival. They asked that God would bring spiritual awakening to their campus and the nation, and also awaken student interest in foreign missions. At this point, the United States was barely 30 years old. International travel was difficult at best and most churches were focused on a local ministry. During one of their meetings, they got caught in a thunderstorm. To get out of the storm they found refuge under a nearby haystack. Under that haystack, their informal leader, Samuel Mills, "invited the students to join with him in offering their lives in the cause of foreign missions."[1] God was honored by the prayers of these young men, and over the next several months, Williams College experienced a great revival that later became known as the "Haystack Revival."

J. Edwin Orr, an expert in spiritual awakenings, explained the tremendous impact of that revival:

> not only Williams College, but also Yale, Amherst, Dartmouth, Princeton, to name a few, reported the conversion of *a third to a half* of their total student bodies, which in those days usually numbered between 100-250.[2]

But that's not all. Within four years of that prayer meeting, Mills, along with several other students, presented a petition to begin North America's first missionary society. A year and a half later, as a direct result of these students' prayers and efforts, a group of recent college graduates became North America's first

---

1   Hayes, Dan. 1995. *Fireseeds of Spiritual Awakening.* Orlando: Campus Crusade for Christ Integrated Resources. P 31
2   (Hayes 1995, 32)

missionaries. Leading out in that first group of missionaries was Adoniram Judson, a missionary to India and Burma.[3]

The vision and passion of Samuel Mills and his friends resulted in hundreds of students coming to faith, a spiritual transformation on several universities, and the launching of a missionary movement in North America that continues on today, impacting the world for Jesus.

So, what are you trusting God for?

I have spent the past 30 years of my life asking people this very question. In 1989, I joined the staff of Campus Crusade for Christ, (today known as Cru in the US, Power to Change in Canada), focusing on impacting college and university students with the gospel. In the course of my various roles in the US, Canada, and several other nations around the world, I have been able to sit across the table from literally thousands of Christians from a wide variety of backgrounds—university students, marketplace leaders, entrepreneurs, politicians, professional athletes, and many others.

Early in my conversations with each of these people, I like to ask them this simple question:

What are you trusting God for?

If I were to sum up the thousands of answers that I have received to that question over the years, it would be with these two words:

"Not much."

Here are a few examples of what I have heard:

"I hope to encourage a few people in their walk with God."

"I'd love if God could one day use me to introduce one person to faith."

"I'd maybe like to lead a Bible study."

---

3   Traveling Team. 2018. "Articles." Haystack Prayer Meeting. Accessed December 1, 2018. http://www.thetravelingteam.org/articles/haystack-prayer-meeting.

Don't Settle

Throughout the Bible, I see God frequently accomplishing the improbable and the impossible. But when I talk with most Christians, I notice a disconnect between how people view the God of the Bible vs. what they are willing to trust God to do. There seems to be a sense of "He used others to do amazing things, but he probably doesn't want to use me." And when people are willing to trust him, it is for relatively small outcomes.

For some Christians, I think these small dreams are connected to a false sense of humility: "I'm nothing special, like the apostle Paul or Billy Graham, so I don't want to have too high expectations." As we will discuss later in the book, the scope of our impact has very little to do with our gifts or abilities, but has everything to do with how we allow God to work through us.

For others, the lack of vision is related to comfort or complacency. These people just want to enjoy the benefits of knowing Jesus, without making a lot of waves. I believe complacency is another word for "disobedience." God has not saved us and left us on earth so we can enjoy a self-serving life. He has much bigger plans for us.

Still others have bought into a Christian cultural mindset that reinforces mediocrity. Let me give you an example of this.

Every culture has clichés that are accepted as fact. In the Christian world, sometimes these clichés can carry more weight than the words of Jesus. One of the cliches that kind of bothers me is this:

If it just touches one, it is worth it.

On the one hand, there is truth to this. Every soul is of infinite value to God, and Jesus emphasized this through his parable of the 99 sheep in Luke 15:4-7.

> Suppose one of you has a hundred sheep and loses one of them. Doesn't he leave the ninety-nine in the open country and go after the lost sheep until he finds it? And when he

finds it, he joyfully puts it on his shoulders and goes home. Then he calls his friends and neighbors together and says, "Rejoice with me; I have found my lost sheep." I tell you that in the same way there will be more rejoicing in heaven over one sinner who repents than over ninety-nine righteous persons who do not need to repent.

So, of course, each individual has great worth. But as we look at the overall mission to which Jesus called his followers, we see that we are called to a far larger vision. If one individual is of incredible worth, then two individuals are worth even more. So what about 1000? Or one million?

You are Called to More

In Matthew 28:18-20, widely known as the Great Commission, Jesus commanded his disciples to "make disciples of **all nations,** teaching them to obey everything I have commanded you" (*emphasis mine*). He said in Acts 1:8 that "You shall be my witnesses in Jerusalem, and in all Judea and Samaria, and to the **ends of the earth.**"

And, of course, in his most famous statement, Jesus said in John 3:16 that "God so loved the **world** that he gave his one and only Son."

In fact, the vision for a global impact by God's people was given from the very beginning of Scripture.

When God called Abram in Genesis 12:2-3, he said,

I will make you into a great nation, and I will bless you; I will make your name great, and you will be a blessing. I will bless those who bless you, and whoever curses you I will curse; and **all peoples on earth will be blessed through you.**

From the very beginning, God gave his people a vision that was global.

We can see from these Scriptures and several others that

God's overarching theme is the redemption of the world. So let's ask him to allow us to play a big part in that!

The World is Waiting

There is another compelling reason why we should seek to have a God-sized vision: there are a lot of serious problems in the world that need God-sized solutions! Let me share a small sample:

- Every year, in North America, there are over three million reports of child abuse. These are just the ones reported![4]
- Every day, 29,000 children die from preventable diseases. That equals more than 10 million children every year.[5]
- Globally, there are about 46 million people who live as slaves (sex slaves, or simply indentured servants).[6]
- There are approximately 153 million orphans in the world today.[7]
- Over 840 million people do not have clean drinking water according to the WHO/Unicef Joint Monitoring Programme (JMP) Report 2017.[8]
- 821 million people go to bed hungry every night.[9]
- In what could be the most tragic statistic when considering the eternal ramifications, there are approximately 3.1 billion people on the planet who have not heard the gospel and, because of cultural, religious, geographic or political reasons, are totally isolated from hearing it.[10] In

4   Child Help. 2018. "Child Abuse Statistics and Facts". Accessed November 30, 2018
    https://www.childhelp.org/child-abuse-statistics/?gclid=EAIaIQobChMIx8aN4fzL3AIVirrACh2SU
    wu8EAAYASAAEgJ6oPD_BwE
5   Unicef. 2015. "Millenium Development Goals". Child Mortality. Accessed December 12, 2018.
    https://www.unicef.org/mdg/childmortality.html
6   Minderoo Foundation, Walk Free. 2019, "What We Do". Accessed Mar 7, 2019.
    https://www.minderoo.com.au/walk-free/
7   SOS Children's Village. 2018. "Worldwide Children's Statistics." Updated April 2018.
    https://www.sos-usa.org/our-impact/childrens-statistics
8   Water Aid. 2018. "WHO/UNICEF Joint Monitoring Programme (JMP) Report 2017". Facts and
    Statistics. Accessed November 1, 2018. https://www.wateraid.org/facts-and-statistics
9   World Food Program. 2018. Zero Hunger. Accessed November 1, 2018.
    http://www1.wfp.org/zero-hunger
10 Joshua Project 2017. "Global Summary an Overview of the People Groups of the World." People
    Groups. Accessed November 1, 2018. https://joshuaproject.net/people_groups/statistics

fact, of those 3.1 billion people, 66,000 die every day without ever having had access to the gospel.[11] That works out to one person every 1.3 seconds.

So . . . what are you trusting God for?

Trust God to Do the Impossible

The God we serve is the all-powerful, all-knowing, sovereign Creator and King of the universe who loves every person he created. He is able to do, according to Ephesians 3:20, "exceeding, abundantly beyond all we can ask or think." (NASB 1977) Why would we be satisfied with touching only a few people when God has commanded us and empowered us to do so much more? Remember that when Jesus gave this command to his disciples, many of them had not traveled further than 30 miles from home. He was not afraid to give them a vision that seemed impossible and that probably made them feel pretty uncomfortable. And yet, this small band of men literally "upset the world" (Acts 17:6, NASB) and began a movement that continues to expand today.

Because we easily forget that God is a God of the impossible, he repeats this idea several times in Scripture:

- "Is anything too hard for the Lord?" (Genesis 18:14)
- "I know that you can do all things." (Job 42:2)
- "I am the LORD, the God of all mankind. Is anything too difficult for me?" (Jeremiah 32:27 NASB)
- "With man this is impossible, but with God all things are possible." (Matthew 19:26)
- "Everything is possible for one who believes." (Mark 9:23)
- "With man this is impossible, but not with God; all things are possible with God." (Mark 10:27)

---

11   One World Mission. 2018. "The Unreached." Resources. Accessed November 30, 2018
     http://oneworldmissions.com/site.cfm?pageid=6064

- "Abba, Father," [Jesus] said, "everything is possible for you." (Mark 14:36)
- "For nothing will be impossible with God." (Luke 1:37 NASB)
- "What is impossible with man is possible with God." (Luke 18:27)

And my favorite,

- "Now to Him who is able to do exceeding, abundantly beyond all that we can ask or imagine." (Ephesians 3:20 NASB 1977)

God wants us to trust him for big things. By trusting him for big things, we are acknowledging that he is able to do big things. And that glorifies him.

Modern Men of God-sized Vision

One of my favorite quotes is: "Attempt something so great for God that it is doomed for failure if He is not in it" (John Haggai). I like to call this a God-sized vision. A God-sized vision is one that we cannot accomplish without him. A God-sized vision forces us to trust him, to be empowered by him, and to pray like crazy to him.

Missionary Hudson Taylor trusted God to see thousands of Chinese come to know Jesus.

Brother Andrew (*God's Smuggler*) trusted God to smuggle Bibles into difficult places right under the noses of the authorities.

Bill Bright, founder of Cru, trusted God to make a movie about the life of Jesus that could be shown to billions of people around the world. *The Jesus Film* is now available in 1670 languages and has been viewed 8.1 billion times, becoming one of the most fruitful and effective evangelistic tools in history.

Apple co-founder Steve Jobs wanted to create technologies that would revolutionize the world.

Wait a minute, Steve Jobs? I threw him in there to highlight that some secular leaders dream big, and many of them see success. In fact, when Jobs was trying to lure John Sculley away from his role as President of Pepsico, Jobs said, "Do you want to sell sugar water the rest of your life or do you want to change the world?"[12]

Now You

Unfortunately, many leaders put huge effort and passion behind creating products that will likely be obsolete in 10-20 years. I am asking that you dream big for God's cause, so that we can impact the eternal destiny of billions of souls for whom Jesus died. I am asking you to dream big because God has given us a massive task with eternal ramifications. We are children of the Almighty King of Kings! We, of all people, should have a God-sized vision.

So, what are you trusting God for?

Let's Get Practical

You may be saying, "I could never dream this big! That's just not who I am."

No matter what your gift set is, I believe you can develop a bigger vision, so I want to help you by providing you with some practical next steps.

I learned a very simple principle in university about a big vision, using the notion of a continuum.

---

12   Signal v. Noise, 2011, https://signalvnoise.com/posts/2813-do-you-want-to-sell-sugar-water-for, accessed Jan 24, 2019

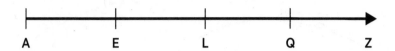

The idea is this: If you start at point A, and are aiming to get to L, you will probably end up at E. But if you only shoot for L, you will probably not ever get past L, and most likely, you will never come close to Q or Z.

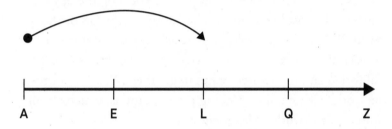

On the other hand, if your objective is to reach Z, then, naturally, you are going to have to go through E, L and Q to get there.

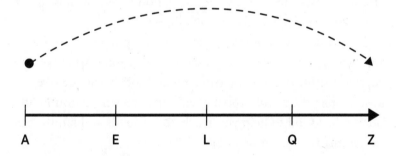

Makes sense, right? Let me give you a practical example of how this works by adding some locations to the line.

Let's say that you are living in Los Angeles, either working in the business world, or maybe studying at UCLA. Los Angeles is located in California, which is a "subset" of the United States, which, in turn, is a part of the world.

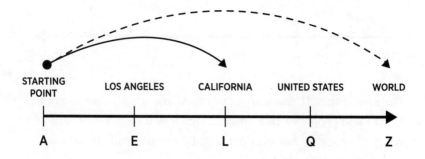

If your aim is to reach Los Angeles, and you stop there, your impact will most likely not reach California, the US or the world. But, if, for example, you are asking God to use you to reach the world, then you have to go through Los Angeles, California and the United States to get there. You cannot reach the world without also reaching these locations, which are all subsets of the world. Make sense?

Let's make this more personal. On the line below, write the name of your local area (university, city, etc.) above the letter E. Above the L, write the state or province in which your local area is located. Then, above Q, write the nation in which those areas are found. I've helped you out by filling in Z!

Now, I want you to take a moment and put an "x" on the point on the line that best represents your vision—what is the scope of the impact you are trusting God for? If you are like most people, the x will probably end up somewhere around "B." You've asked God to help you reach your friends and family, but you haven't thought much beyond that.

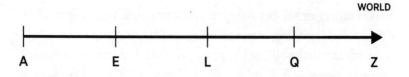

My guess is that Jesus' disciples were pretty similar to us in this way. They were small-town people who had likely never considered life outside of their local community. But Jesus wanted to give them a God-sized vision. In Acts 1:8, which occurs just after the resurrection, and just before Jesus ascended to heaven, Jesus expanded the disciples' vision. He said, "But you will receive power when the Holy Spirit comes on you; and you will be my witnesses in Jerusalem, and in all Judea and Samaria, and to the ends of the earth."

Placing these locations on the same continuum, you can see that Jesus was pushing out the vision of the disciples' ministry to ultimately reach the entire world.

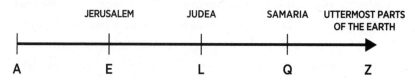

First, Jesus tells his disciples that they will be witnesses in Jerusalem. This was probably bigger than they had been thinking, but it was not too much of a stretch because the disciples were familiar with Jerusalem. They knew the area, which was close by, and likely had a lot of friends and family there.

Then, Jesus says, they are to be witnesses in Judea. Judea was a province that included the cities of Jerusalem, Jericho and Bethlehem. Culturally, this was a Jewish area, so there was still some familiarity and comfort.

Samaria was made up of a group of people who were considered enemies to the Jews. This implied not only cross-cultural ministry, but reaching out to people who hated them!

Finally, Jesus tells his disciples that they are to be witnesses "to the uttermost parts of the earth." That pretty much covers everyone else in the world.

Jesus did not shy away from giving his 12 young followers this command, and in fact, he was giving it to you and me

as well. Why do I say that? Let's look again at the Great
Commission in Matthew 28:18-20.

> And Jesus came to them and said, "All authority in heaven
> and on earth has been given to me. Therefore go therefore
> and make disciples of **all nations,** baptizing them in the name
> of the Father and of the Son and of the Holy Spirit, and
> **teaching them to obey everything I have commanded you.**
> And surely I am with you always, to the very end of the age."

Jesus' command to his disciples was to not only make disciples
of all nations (a God-sized vision), but also to teach their disciples "to obey **all** I have commanded you"—which includes his
command to make disciples of all nations! In other words, the
Great Commission was not just given to those 12 men, but to
every believer in every generation. That is a God-sized task. So
let me give you five practical steps to help you develop a God-
sized vision in order to have a God-sized impact.

1. Expand Your Vision

The first step is establishing the scope of your vision. How do we
get a God-sized vision? Simply ask God for a big vision. While
some people are naturally visionary, most of us need God to
help us with this. So ask him! Matthew 7:7-8 says,

> Ask and it will be given to you; seek and you will find; knock
> and the door will be opened to you. For everyone who asks
> receives; the one who seeks finds; and to the one who knocks,
> the door will be opened.

James 4:2 says that we don't have because we don't ask. So ask
him. Go ahead and begin praying that God expands your vision.

2. Memorize Big-God Verses

Second, look for, meditate on, and memorize what I would call "big-God" verses. My favorite is Ephesians 3:20, which I shared earlier. Maybe start with some of the verses I shared a couple of pages back. Look up passages that talk about how God spoke the universe into being and holds it together. Study verses that talk about him raising Jesus from the dead or how he controls the outcome of history. This is a God of whom we can ask big things! It is important that we internalize what the Bible says about who God is and what he is able to do, so that we will be more willing to ask him for things that are commensurate with his power.

3. Stimulate Your Mind

Third, expand your vision through educating yourself. I try to regularly read books that inspire me with what God is doing or has done. Every believer can benefit from reading classic missionary biographies such as *God's Smuggler*, *Through Gates of Splendor*, and *Hudson Taylor's Spiritual Secret*. More recently I have been inspired by books such as *Dreams and Visions* by Tom Doyle, which tells stories of Muslims encountering Jesus and coming to faith through dreams. Brother Andrew's book, *Secret Believers*, tells stories of how God is moving throughout the Muslim world, and Randy Alcorn's *Safely Home* tells a story related to the explosive growth of the church in China.

I would also encourage you to explore and utilize online resources such as Operation World, Joshua Project and the US Center for World Missions. These sites offer tons of information about the current state of the Great Commission and the needs of the world. They offer numerous resources, stories and statistics to expand your vision.

I have also found that secular books can inspire me to dream bigger. The stories about companies such as Starbucks, Apple and Google can also be vision-expanding. Steve Jobs, Elon Musk, Mark Zuckerberg and others have taken the world in new directions (whatever you might think about the value of those directions) with their big thinking and innovation. We can learn from their willingness to dream big. On occasion, I even read magazines such as *Wired* or *Popular Science* to expand my thinking about what could be possible. These can stimulate your mind to dream bigger.

4. Spend Time with "Big God" People

A fourth key is spending time with visionaries and people who are stepping out in faith. If you want to be a "Big God" type of person, hang around people who are "Big God" people. Cynics and skeptics have never accomplished much for the Kingdom, so, generally, I avoid people like that. Seek out godly, faith-filled people who are willing to trust God for big things. These are the types of people who see him use them for big things. So seek out people who will encourage you to dream big for God.

When I was at Baylor, Louie Giglio was leading a Bible study for a small group of students. Louie is a "Big God" person, and in his teaching, he constantly reminded us that the God we serve is an awesome, all-powerful, amazing God! I not only attended Louie's Bible study, but I sought to spend time with him individually, and to learn all I could about God from him. Today, Louie is pastor of Passion City Church, and has a ministry that has touched millions of people all over the world. Hanging around "Big God" people like Louie will inevitably expand your faith and help expand your Kingdom impact.

5. Build Your Faith

Finally, acknowledge that **the realities of the past are the possibilities of our future.** If God did it before, he can do it again! So, become an expert on the ways in which God moved supernaturally in the past. Do a study on supernatural occurrences in the Bible, such as God delivering the Israelites out of Egypt, or Daniel and his friends, or the growth of the early church in Acts.

Personally, I have been incredibly moved by what God did through the Student Volunteer Movement, which started with 100 students consecrating themselves to foreign missions in 1899 that eventually mobilized over 15,000 missionaries all over the world. The "grandchildren" of this movement include InterVarsity, the Navigators and Cru.

Read about spiritual awakenings that have happened over the past 500 years. Study the lives of great evangelists such as D.L. Moody, John Wesley and Billy Graham. These stories will inspire you to trust God for bigger things.

The God we serve loves you and me so much, that he sent his Son to die for us. Our God is all-powerful, all-knowing, and sovereign over all things. He has given us a huge task and his Holy Spirit to accomplish this task (more on that in the next chapter). This is a God of whom we can ask great things.

So . . . what are you trusting God for?

CHAPTER 2

Supernatural Power

Popeye The Sailor Man

When I was a kid, I watched a lot of Popeye cartoons. For those of you who don't know, Popeye the Sailor was a funny looking and sounding guy who was a bit of a pushover—until he ate his spinach. He would face some danger or menace, and just when it looked like he was done for, he would grab a can of spinach, swallow the whole thing in one gulp, and become transformed into an unstoppable fighting machine. Once he had consumed this "wonder veg," nobody could stop him. He would acquire the strength of twenty men and take down any threat.

Popeye was one of the most popular cartoons in the 1930s. In fact, when the Popeye cartoon first came out around the time of the Great Depression, spinach sales in the US jumped by 33%. Everyone wanted that extra power!

But there has always been one nagging question that has bothered me about Popeye: if spinach gave him this extraordinary strength, and he knew that without spinach, he was a wimp, why didn't he just eat spinach all day long? I mean, why would Popeye allow himself to get beaten up by bullies when he had easy access to this superfood that would eliminate any threat he encountered?

If I were Popeye, and I knew that spinach gave me this amazing power, I would do everything I could to ensure that spinach was a regular part of my diet. I would have spinach omelets for breakfast, spinach quiche for lunch, spinach salad for dinner and spinach smoothies throughout the day. Wouldn't that make sense?

I think that often, we Christians are just like a spinach-deprived Popeye. We have access to this supernatural power, but we choose to live our lives without tapping into it. Like Popeye, when we lack this power source, we are easily defeated. But when we tap into God's power, we are able to take on greater challenges. In the cartoon world of Popeye, that power source was spinach. In our real world, Jesus has provided us access to his supernatural power through his Holy Spirit. And unlike Popeye's spinach, the Holy Spirit indwells every person who has placed their faith in Jesus Christ. His power is available to us at any time! As we are trusting God to have a Kingdom-impact that is "exceeding, abundantly beyond all we can ask or imagine," it is imperative that we understand that Jesus never expected us to have this impact through our own power or strength. The only way that we can have a God-sized impact on our world is through the power of God's Holy Spirit.

Help Needed

Jesus knew that after his ascension to heaven, the disciples would have many struggles. He knew that their fears, insecurities and sinful nature would limit their ability to carry out his mission. He knew that they would face intense opposition and persecution, and that, on their own, they would be incapable of standing strong and growing his church. And so he promised to send them help.

In John 14:16-17, he says,

> And I will ask the Father, and he will give you another advocate to help you and be with you forever—the Spirit of truth. The world cannot accept him, because it neither sees him nor knows him. But you know him, for he lives with you and will be in you.

This is an amazing promise!

After the resurrection and before his ascension, Jesus spent
about 40 days with the disciples. During that time, he reiterated
his promise that he would send help. In Luke 24:49, he tells his
disciples,

> I am going to send you what my Father has promised; but
> stay in the city until you have been clothed with power from
> on high.

Jesus expands on the idea in Acts 1:8,

> But you will receive power when the Holy Spirit comes on
> you; and you will be my witnesses in Jerusalem, and in all
> Judea and Samaria, and to the ends of the earth.

In both of these statements, Jesus uses the word "power." Jesus
promised that the Holy Spirit would come on them, and
they would be "clothed" with power. What type of power?
Resurrection power! Listen to what the Apostle Paul says in
Ephesians 1:18-20:

> I pray that the eyes of your heart may be enlightened in order
> that you may know the hope to which he has called you, the
> riches of his glorious inheritance in his holy people, and his
> incomparably great power for us who believe. That power is
> the same as the mighty strength he exerted when he raised
> Christ from the dead and seated him at his right hand in the
> heavenly realms.

The Holy Spirit indwells every believer from the moment that
they receive Jesus' gift of salvation through faith. However, many
Christians never allow the Holy Spirit to do his work in their
lives. The Holy Spirit, with his supernatural power, is eager to
help us live an abundant Christian life, and allow us to have an
outsized spiritual impact. We simply need to tap into his power,
like a branch taps into a vine to bear fruit.

Bear Much Fruit

John 15:1-5 is a remarkable passage of Scripture. In this passage, Jesus explains his desire for us to produce "much fruit."

> I am the true vine, and my Father is the gardener. He cuts off every branch in me that bears no fruit, while every branch that does **bear fruit** he prunes so that it will be **even more fruitful**. You are already clean because of the word I have spoken to you. Remain in me, as I also remain in you. No branch can **bear fruit** by itself; it must remain in the vine. Neither can you bear fruit unless you remain in me. I am the vine; you are the branches. If you remain in me and I in you, you will **bear much fruit**; apart from me you can do nothing.

Several years ago, my wife and I were on a summer missions project in a Middle Eastern country, sharing the gospel with Muslim university students. The home that we had rented was a simple apartment that was situated behind the main house of the owner. At the front of the owner's house was a trellis, which was covered with a beautiful grape vine. During our four weeks in this apartment, we walked past this grape vine every day, watching the very beginnings of grape clusters starting to grow. Unfortunately, we were never able to enjoy the fruit of this vine because we had to head home a few weeks before the grapes were fully ripe and ready to enjoy. But we knew that when the time was right, there would be hundreds of succulent grapes for all to enjoy. That's a lot of fruit!

Now let's imagine going back to the time when the owner of our place first purchased his grapevine. He buys a small grapevine, takes it home and selects the best location to maximize the fruitfulness of this vine. He ensures that it is positioned to get enough sunlight, and is not overtaken by other plants or trees. He builds a trellis next to it to guide the vine as it begins to grow. He learns that it usually takes about three years for a grapevine to begin to produce grapes that are viable and great-tasting, so during that time, he patiently waters the plant, gives it fertilizer, and protects it against animals that may destroy it. As the end of year three approaches, he knows that the time to enjoy the fruit is close. He gathers all of his friends and family together around his precious grapevine and excitedly makes this proclamation:

"Over the next five years, I am really hoping that this grapevine produces 10-15 really quality grapes."

Sounds kind of silly, doesn't it?

When someone plants a grapevine, the expectation is that it will produce a LOT of fruit over its lifetime. None of us would be satisfied with a grapevine that produced just a few grapes a year. In the same way, Jesus tells us that as we abide in him, when we are accessing his power, we should expect to see a lot of fruit produced!

This is part of the reason that I am uncomfortable with the "if it just touches one" mindset. Yes, we need to rejoice when even one person comes to faith, but from Jesus' teachings, we can see that he has a much bigger vision for our Kingdom impact. We can expect that he can use us to produce "much fruit!"

Consider these statements from Jesus:

- "This is to my Father's glory, that you **bear much fruit,** showing yourselves to be my disciples." (John 15:8)
- "You did not choose me, but I chose you and appointed you so that you might go and **bear fruit**—fruit that will last—and so that whatever you ask in my name the Father will give you." (John 15:16)
- "Truly, truly, I say to you, unless a grain of wheat falls into the earth and dies, it remains alone; but if it dies, it **bears much fruit.**" (John 12:24 NASB)

And one of the most incredible promises made by Jesus is found in John 14:12:

- "Very truly I tell you, whoever believes in me will do the

works I have been doing, and they will do greater things
than these, because I am going to the Father."

One of the main reasons that Jesus has given us his Holy Spirit
is **so that** he can empower us to have an incredibly fruitful
ministry! I believe he can use every one of us to have a massive,
God-sized impact: not because of our gifts or hard work, but
because of the power of his Holy Spirit.

Apart From Me, You Can Do Nothing

Another truth I want to point out comes at the end of John 15:5
when Jesus says, "If you remain in me and I in you, you will
bear much fruit; apart from me you can do nothing."

A couple of years ago, as I was reading through this passage,
this statement really jumped out at me: apart from Jesus, I can't
do anything! I can't unconditionally love my neighbors or my
family. I can't consistently live a life of purity or obedience. I
can't have any kind of lasting Kingdom impact.

In Acts 17:28, Paul says, "In him we live and move and have
our being." Apart from Jesus, I can do nothing! The longer I
walk with Jesus and the longer I am in ministry, the more I
recognize the truth of this statement. Let me tell you a story
about how I came to understand this in my life.

When I first started engaging in ministry, I was in way over my
head. I was unsure how to have a personal ministry. A steady
flow of mistakes kept me teachable and dependent upon God.
However, after a decade of ministry experience and training, I
was feeling pretty confident in my leadership and abilities. There
were a lot of ministry tasks that I was able to do "with my eyes
closed" because I had done them so many times—prepare talks,
recruit a student to a project, share my faith, etc. However, at
times, I discovered that when I tried to do these things apart

from the Holy Spirit's empowering, my words would fall flat
and I wasn't very effective. I would spend a day meeting with
students on campus and have really nothing to show for it. Or,
worse, I would offend or hurt people because I was trying to do
things out of the strength of my personality.

This all came to a head for me in 2001. I was in charge of a
summer missions project in Canada, and we were having one of
the best national projects that I can remember. We had one of
the largest groups of students that we had ever had on a national
project. We had a great staff team, that was having a lot of fun
together. Students were getting a vision for the world, sharing
their faith, etc. Everything was going well.

That summer, we had a few students who I felt had some
"teachability issues." I decided that I would "help" them adjust
their attitudes and get them back on track. During the last week
that the staff were on the project (students would take over after
we left), I confronted a student on what I thought was a recur-
ring attitude issue. I felt this student was ignoring our repeated
requests about a minor issue, and so I wanted to deal with it before we let the students take over. There was a sweet young staff
woman I'll call Suzie who felt that he was not listening to her, so
I arranged a meeting for the three of us, where I would confront
this student and get the situation straightened out. During that
confrontation, I was frustrated with the student's response and
so I blew up at him. At the time, I felt justified, but I was wrong.
I had lost control and although I did not physically touch him, I
spoke harshly to him and treated him poorly and disrespectfully.

A week later, I was on vacation, and I received one of those
"what happened?" calls from our national director. He had heard
about the situation, which he said did not sound good. He
wanted to hear my side of the story. From our conversation, I
not only feared that I was in trouble, but became concerned that
I might lose my job. Another veteran staff leader was assigned
to help me "adjust my attitude" (ironic, eh?), and to ensure that

I would make things right with the student against whom I had sinned. I apologized to the student and to others who were impacted by my actions. It was embarrassing, humbling, and not fun.

One of the most painful parts of this pertained to the young staff woman, Suzie. Suzie was caught in the middle of a difficult situation, and she was understandably upset by the whole ordeal. She had relayed to my director that, several times throughout that confrontation, I had "gotten mad" and spoken angrily to the student. Though it may not have been directly as a result of my actions that day, a few weeks after that incident, Suzie resigned from our staff. I still feel badly about that today, because I am sure my response to that young man contributed to her decision to leave our staff. Coming out of that situation, I was humiliated, upset, and my confidence was completely shaken. I felt like a complete failure.

Later that summer, I was at our staff conference in Colorado when Bill Bright, founder and then-president of Cru, encouraged all of our staff to prayerfully consider going on a 40-day fast.

Fasting is an excellent spiritual exercise that allows you to put aside food for a period of time in order to focus more intensely on your relationship with God, and in this case, consuming only liquids for 40 days.

My wife, Joanne, had really wanted to do an extended fast like this, but I had been resistant, mainly because, well, I like food. Now, however, I was ready to take this step of faith so God could work in my heart.

On the very first day of that fast, I was at our church during our regular service. We were in the middle of our worship time when I heard someone from behind me say:

"It's not about you, it's about me."

The words were so clear, that I turned around to see who had said them to me. But when I looked, there were only a few women there, who were completely enthralled in the worship time, with their eyes closed. This was one of those very rare occasions where I have actually heard directly from God.

That very brief message profoundly impacted my walk with God and approach to ministry. For much of my prior ministry career, I had been working out of my own strength, trying to achieve great things in *my* power with *my* natural gifts, so that people would be impressed with *me*. I had been able to get away with it . . . for a while. But eventually, my natural abilities created more frustration and grief than lasting fruit.

In a lot of ways, that statement is a perfect summation of the Spirit-filled life. It is not about me or you, it is about Jesus. And if the work is about him, then that would mean that the work should be done **through** him and **by** him, and ultimately **for** him. Paul says as much in Romans 11:36: "For from him and through him and for him are all things. To him be glory forever!"

The following fall, I went back to my ministry with a deepened sense of dependency on God to do the work. When I went on ministry appointments, I would, almost in fear, beg God to allow me to be used. I didn't want to hurt anybody else, and I certainly didn't want to discourage people in their faith and ministry. I had gained a realization that I desperately needed God to do the work if I was going to see lasting fruit, and not cause damage.

Today, before I go into any ministry meetings with individuals or groups, I find myself acknowledging my need for God to empower me with his Spirit and wisdom. Before I speak at churches or weekly meetings, I confess to God my complete inability to offer anything of value apart from his Spirit.

I am actually at my best when I live under the reality that "apart from Jesus, I can do nothing."

Power for Daily Living

Day-to-day Power

There are a variety of ways of expressing this concept—being filled with the Spirit, partnering with the Spirit, walking with the Spirit, living a Christ-centered life, etc.—but in all cases the ultimate aim is that we depend on God rather than on our own strength to help us live the Christian life. All of these models may have slightly different emphases, but here is how I came to understand it in a way that has impacted me deeply.

Being filled (directed and empowered) with the Holy Spirit is a moment-by-moment lifestyle, allowing Jesus to live through me in every aspect of my life. Abiding in Christ allows me to eliminate the "I shoulds" in my life and replace them with a faith-filled dependence upon the Holy Spirit to do his work in and through me.

When I was a younger Christian, I used to think, "I invited Jesus into my life by grace through faith. But from that point forward, it is all up to me." I had a long list of "shoulds" that drove my performance-based life:

- **I should** work hard to spend time reading the Word and praying every day.
- **I should** work up the courage to share my faith with others who don't know Jesus.
- **I should** choose to love people whom I really don't like that much.

Paul had some strong words for the Galatians who had a similar attitude:

> You foolish Galatians! Who has bewitched you? Before your very eyes Jesus Christ was clearly portrayed as crucified. I would like to learn just one thing from you: Did you receive the Spirit by the works of the law, or by believing what you heard? Are you so foolish? After beginning by means of the

Spirit, are you now trying to finish by means of the flesh? (Galatians 3:1-3)

Paul was reminding his readers that the Holy Spirit is to empower every part of our lives—from the day we came to faith until he takes us home to heaven. To best enjoy my walk with Jesus and my ministry, I need to consistently trust in the Holy Spirit to work in and through me in every aspect of my life.

I remember talking once to a long-serving and fruitful ministry leader about how he kept up with the pace and the responsibilities of his job. I was constantly amazed at all he was able to juggle, and I became fearful and overwhelmed when I thought of taking on more ministry responsibilities.

"How do you keep going and handle all that is on your plate?" I asked.

His reply was simple and profound: "Every day, I ask the Holy Spirit to give me the power to do what he's called me to do that day." I found that incredibly helpful! There have been so many days when I have been too tired or discouraged or over-whelmed or guilty to go on. In those times, I am learning—by faith—to allow the Holy Spirit to give me the power to carry on.

The "Want To"

Beyond recognizing that apart from Christ I can do nothing, I'm also learning that apart from the filling of the Holy Spirit, I don't even **want** to walk with Jesus and to be involved in ministry. I need the Holy Spirit to keep me motivated in my walk with God and ministry.

Paul says in Philippians 2:12-13 NASB,

> So then, my beloved, just as you have always obeyed, not as in my presence only, but now much more in my absence, work out your salvation with fear and trembling; for it is God who is at work in you, both to will and to work for His good pleasure.

I have heard this verse used to talk about the importance of us "working out our salvation." But what I love about this verse is the idea that "it is God who is at work in you, both to will and to work." God is at work in me, giving me the will (the desire) and the work (he's working ahead of me).

I need God to constantly fill me so that I actually want to follow and serve him. Otherwise, I will focus exclusively on me and my selfish desires. I need God to give me a heart for the lost and the courage to share my faith with them. I need the Holy Spirit to give me a hunger for his Word and to help me. I need the Holy Spirit to help me want to love and serve my family better. This changes my "shoulds" into "want tos."

Power To Overcome My Fears and Inadequacies

The Holy Spirit also enables me to take on challenges that are outside of my comfort zone. In my role today, I am involved in working with very successful people from the worlds of business, politics and sports. In fact, everyone I work with is smarter than me, more successful than me, and a lot wealthier than me. It can be an intimidating group of people to work with! Additionally, I am responsible to help raise money for our ministry. While I enjoy this, I can feel a fair bit of pressure at times to "deliver the goods." But I have learned that this is a great place for me to be, because I am regularly forced out of my comfort zone, which then forces me to be increasingly reliant upon the Holy Spirit.

Two Types Of Fruit

Fruit of the Spirit

There are two types of fruit that the Holy Spirit empowers me to bear—fruit of the Spirit and fruit of ministry. Let's start with fruit of the Spirit.

In Galatians 5:17, Paul contrasts the fruit of the flesh with the fruit of the Spirit, explaining that they are battling against one another.

> For the flesh desires what is **contrary** to the Spirit, and the Spirit what is **contrary** to the flesh. They are in **conflict** with each other, so that you are not to do whatever you want."

He then goes on to describe the acts of the flesh in graphic detail in verses 19-21:

> The acts of the flesh are obvious: sexual immorality, impurity and debauchery; idolatry and witchcraft; hatred, discord, jealousy, fits of rage, selfish ambition, dissensions, factions and envy; drunkenness, orgies, and the like. I warn you, as I did before, that those who live like this will not inherit the kingdom of God.

When we look at that list, it makes sense as to why our world is in such a mess. War, crime, abuse, and the biggest problems in the world all flow from these fruits of the flesh. The scary thing is when I allow my flesh to control my life, I bear this type of nasty fruit.

In contrast, in verses 22-23 (NASB), Paul says that "the fruit of the Spirit is love, joy, peace, patience, kindness, goodness, faithfulness, gentleness, self-control; against such things there is no law."

The fruit that is produced in me depends on who is in control—my flesh or the Holy Spirit.

Take a moment and think about what the world would look like if the vast majority of believers developed a habit of

regularly abiding in Christ by being filled with the Holy Spirit.
Imagine the impact!

- Divorce rates and marital affairs would decrease dramat-
  ically as sexual immorality, impurity, jealousy, and fits of
  rage are replaced by love, peace, patience, faithfulness and
  self-control.
- Church splits would be radically reduced as selfish ambition, dissensions and factions are replaced by love, peace,
  patience and gentleness.
- The poor would be better looked after as Christians
  prioritize demonstrating the love, goodness and kindness
  of God to meet their needs.
- Non-Christians would be attracted by the difference that
  Jesus makes in a person's life as the Holy Spirit bears the
  fruit of love, joy, peace, kindness and goodness in the lives
  of his followers on a more regular basis.

If we want to have a significant Kingdom impact, we need
to allow the Spirit to reign and produce his fruit in our lives.
Additionally, as we help other believers apply this to their lives,
we will multiply the impact we can have through them. We'll
talk more about multiplication in chapter 7.

Ministry Fruit

The second type of fruit that we will bear when we are
empowered by the Holy Spirit is significant ministry fruit.

I think it is telling that Luke, at the very beginning of his
investigative report, the book of Acts, focuses on the connection
that Jesus made between evangelism and the filling of the Spirit.
"But you will receive power when the Holy Spirit comes on you;
and you will be my witnesses in Jerusalem, and in all Judea and
Samaria, and to the ends of the earth." (Acts 1:8).

As we can see here, one of the primary reasons that Jesus

gave us his Holy Spirit is so that we can be his witnesses. And did you notice the scope of the impact Jesus promises here? He promises his disciples that their ministry will reach the ends of the earth! We have been given that same power and that same command, so we too can expect to have a global impact if we allow him to use us. Isn't that incredible?!

Massive Ministry Fruit!

Immediately following the apostles' initial filling of the Holy Spirit at Pentecost in Acts 2, Peter stood up and began to share the gospel. Luke recorded that, at that time, there were people from 15 different nations present, and that over 3000 came to faith that day. That is some serious fruit! And as you read the book of Acts, you can see that the scope of their impact touched Jerusalem, Judea, to Samaria, and the world (Acts 17:6), just as Jesus promised.

A few chapters later, in Acts 4, the apostles faced severe persecution and threats from the authorities. Their response? "After they prayed, the place where they were meeting was shaken. And they were all filled with the Holy Spirit and spoke the word of God boldly." (Acts 4:31).

God filled them and then they boldly proclaimed the gospel.

As you read through the book of Acts, you can see the growth and scope of their Kingdom impact as documented by Luke:

"And the Lord added to their number daily those who were
    being saved." Acts 2:47
"But many who heard the message believed; so the number of
    men who believed grew to about five thousand." Acts 4:4
"So the word of God spread. The number of disciples in
    Jerusalem increased rapidly, and a large number of priests
    became obedient to the faith." Acts 6:7

In other words, their impact expanded to the priesthood.

"But the word of God continued to spread and flourish."
Acts 12:24
"A great number of Jews and Greeks believed." Acts 14:1
"So the churches were strengthened in the faith and grew daily
in numbers." Acts 16:5
"These men who have turned the world upside down have
come here also." Acts 17:6 (ESV)

Wouldn't you love to see that kind of an impact?

We need the Holy Spirit's power to give us motivation and
boldness (the "want to"), wisdom in sharing the gospel and in
making disciples of all nations.

Let's Get Practical

How Are We Filled With The Holy Spirit?

So how do we do this? As Christians, how do we allow the Holy
Spirit to control our lives?

Confession
The first step is to confess our sins to God. When we first came
to Christ, all of our sins were forgiven through Jesus' sacrificial
death on the cross. However, unconfessed sin creates a barrier
in our relationship with God. By confessing our sin—simply
agreeing with God that we sinned—we can restore our fellowship with God and more fully access the Holy Spirit's power in
our lives. I John 1:9 says, "If we confess our sins, he is faithful
and just and will forgive us our sins and purify us from all
unrighteousness."

Confession, on the one hand, is pretty straightforward. I
simply acknowledge my sin to God. He knows I sinned. I know
that I sinned. So we simply agree on that fact. However, confession is made difficult by our pride, which doesn't like to admit
that we have sinned. I don't know about you, but I am often like

a three-year-old child whose face and hands are covered with chocolate, trying to convince my parents that I didn't eat any chocolate cookies. I hate to admit when I sin! Or I try to soft-sell my sin: "I wasn't mad, I was just frustrated." But God wants us to honestly confess our sins, acknowledging that what we did was wrong. And this confession should involve repentance—a change in my attitudes and actions.

Yielding Control

After we have confessed our sin, we now need to affirm God's lordship over our lives. This can also be difficult, because we all like to think that we have control over our lives. But ultimately, control is a myth. I can't control the economy, natural disasters, terrorist attacks, cancer or any number of other things. So it makes sense for me to yield my life to the One who is in control of the universe.

During my last year in high school, my youth leader challenged us to give God complete control of our lives. That idea scared me to death! I liked having "control" over my life and was having a pretty good time in high school. I was having success on my basketball team and getting to go out with some beautiful young ladies. Life was pretty good! I didn't want to give my life over to God—he'd mess things up!

But just before my last semester in high school, I finally took that step. I decided to yield control of my life to Jesus; I would seek to obey his Word and do his will. It had occurred to me that giving the Holy Spirit control of my life was actually the most self-serving action I could take. I am giving control of my life to my all-powerful Creator, my Abba Father, who loves me with an infinite and perfect love, who sent his Son to die for me. Because he loves me perfectly and because he causes all things to work together for good, I can trust that his decisions are only for my best interest. Yielding to his Lordship is the best decision I ever made and continue to make on a regular basis!

Filled By Faith

The final step is asking the Holy Spirit, by faith, to fill us and empower us. This is not an emotional experience, but rather an act of faith. In faith, we simply ask the Holy Spirit to fill us, empower us and take control of our lives.

Inevitably, because of our sinful flesh, we will disobey God and/or take the control of our lives back from him. Once we recognize that we have done this, we simply need to begin this process over again. A good word picture is called spiritual breathing. We "exhale," confessing and repenting of our sins. Then we "inhale" again, asking in faith for the Holy Spirit to fill us and empower us. While the Holy Spirit indwells all believers from the moment of spiritual birth, we are filled (directed and empowered) when we yield control of our lives to him and ask him to fill us by faith. I find that I need to practice spiritual breathing on a regular basis, because, on a regular basis, I disobey God with my thoughts, words or actions.

Why Aren't We Filled With The Spirit?

So why don't most of us experience more of God's power in our lives? I think there are a few reasons.

The first one is unconfessed sin.

Every time I sin, I am asserting control over my life. By not confessing it, I am stubbornly demonstrating that I don't want God to forgive me or take control. This willful disobedience prevents the Holy Spirit from taking control and doing his work in our lives. But we can overcome this by simply admitting our sin and yielding our lives to the Holy Spirit's control.

Another issue that I mentioned earlier is the "I should" problem.

Though following this list of "shoulds" seems noble to many people, it is actually a manifestation of pride. We are essentially saying that our sanctification and ministry fruit will come as a result of our efforts, not the Holy Spirit's. We come to the conclusion that it is my hard work, discipline and perseverance that will accomplish God's purposes. But this runs counter to Jesus' assertion, that "apart from me, you can do nothing." We will bear much fruit only when we abide in Christ, being filled and controlled by the Holy Spirit.

When my kids were young and we were travelling, they would occasionally try to help by picking up one of our heavy suitcases. I would step back and let them try, while ensuring they would not hurt themselves in the process. In their naive self-confidence, they would grunt and struggle, but inevitably fail to even budge the too-heavy burden. At that point, they would grudgingly step back and ask me to carry the suitcase. Then I would effortlessly (sometimes!) pick up and carry the suitcase to where it needed to go.

In a lot of ways, I think God looks at us like kids trying to do more than we can handle. God says, "So you'd like to carry that burden? Sure, if you like, but it's too heavy for you. I'll wait here until you are ready for me to take over." Eventually, we get to the point when we give in and ask God to take over. But we'd save ourselves a lot of pain and struggle if we regularly acknowledged that "apart from Jesus, we can do nothing."

Zechariah 4:6 says, "So he said to me, 'This is the word of the LORD to Zerubbabel: "Not by might, nor by power, but by my Spirit," says the LORD Almighty.'"

In other words, it's not by my natural gifting. Not by my experience or training. Not by my willpower or discipline. But by God's Holy Spirit.

Submitting Ourselves Daily To God's Control.

I have a friend who has walked with Jesus for over 40 years, and has had a very fruitful ministry. Recently, he shared with me his habit of daily giving control of his life to Jesus. Every day, he prays something like this:

> Heavenly Father, today I *need* your work in my life. I place myself completely in your hands to do with as you wish for this day, for apart from you I can do *nothing*. I hold nothing back. Fill *every* area of my body, soul and spirit with your Holy Spirit. Anything you desire to do *to* me and *through* me, do it. If there are areas of my life that I am holding back, invade them anyway. If there are sins I need to confess, reveal them to me. I present my body as a living sacrifice to you. Complete the good work that you have begun in me by your Spirit. Thank you my Lord, my God, and my Redeemer. In the name of Jesus Christ I ask these things. Amen.

God wants us to access his Holy Spirit's power so that we can be used to impact the world for his glory. As we discuss more practical steps in these next several chapters, there is an assumption that none of these things will happen unless the Holy Spirit is driving us. Because, apart from him, we can do nothing. The more we give God control of our lives, the more "useable" we become, allowing us to have an even greater impact.

CHAPTER 3

Our Most Dangerous Weapon

"Father, I pray that my friend Gary would give $100 million to Kingdom priorities."

I wrote that request in my prayer journal in the fall of 2016. Gary (not his real name) and I had been friends for about three years at that point, and we had recently shared some great conversations about a vision to impact the world. Gary had seen tremendous success in business and had given some large gifts to educational institutions and a few other worthy causes. I knew he desired to be used by God to have an impact for the Kingdom, so I decided to begin praying that—over his lifetime—Gary would invest a large amount of his resources in advancing God's work around the world. I wasn't sure if or how God would answer that prayer, but I was going to begin praying and see how God would move.

Have you ever prayed an audacious or outlandish prayer? This prayer of mine was one of the craziest I had ever prayed. But I had seen God do many amazing things over my life, so my faith had grown to the point where I was comfortable praying like this. Let me share some of how I got to this point.

The Faith/Prayer Connection

Throughout history, there have been many heroes of the faith. We have biblical heroes such as Moses, Elijah, Daniel, and the Apostle Paul. I love these guys! They were people of great faith, but they were also people of great prayer. Wouldn't you love to have a Kingdom impact like them?

Moses spent hours and often days with God on Mt. Sinai.

Elijah had that great battle with the prophets of Baal on Mt. Carmel, and his prayers started and ended a drought. Daniel regularly prayed three times a day, even when threatened with being thrown to the lions. Paul spent much of his time in prison singing and praying, and he encouraged us in II Thessalonians 5:17 to "pray without ceasing."

We see this same discipline among great Christian leaders throughout history. In E.M. Bounds' classic book, *Power Through Prayer,* he quotes Martin Luther as saying,

> If I fail to spend two hours in prayer each morning, the devil gets victory through the day. I have so much business I cannot get on without spending three hours daily in prayer.[1]

John Wesley, founder of the Methodist church, is known to have prayed two hours every day, and said,

> Give me one hundred preachers who fear nothing but sin and desire nothing but God, and I care not a straw whether they be clergymen or laymen; such alone will shake the gates of hell and set up the kingdom of heaven on earth. God does nothing but in answer to prayer.[2]

Wesley further said, "I have so much to do that I spend several hours in prayer before I am able to do it."[3]

One of Billy Graham's associates described the prayer life of the great 20th century American evangelist like this:

> When Billy got up this morning, he started praying in his room; he prayed during breakfast and in the car on the way over to the studio; he is praying right now and will continue throughout the interview. Let's just say that Billy keeps himself 'prayed up' all the time.[4]

And yet, when he was asked what he would do if he could start

---

1   Bounds, E.M. 2016. The *Complete Works of EM Bounds.* Dancing Unicorn Books. Kindle edition, location 468
2   Ibid. Kindle location 909
3   Wordpress. (2018). "Prayers of John Wesley". November 30, 2018. http://1dsuj3nnx8w25giyu3oefy11. wpengine.netdna-cdn.com/wp-content/uploads/Prayers-of-John-Wesley.pdf
4   Ross, Larry. 2018. "The Billy Graham I Knew". Time (New York) February 21, 2018. http://time. com/5168915/billy-graham-larry-ross-remembrance

over, Billy said, "I would spend more time in prayer, not just for myself but for others."[5]

The question that comes to my mind is: Do these men pray a lot because they are great men of faith? Or are they great men of faith because they pray a lot?

Well, the answer to this question is . . . yes. It's both!

Prayer and faith are indelibly tied together: the effectiveness of one is directly proportional to the effectiveness of the other.

Let me show you how.

The Cycle Of Prayer

You may have heard of the cycle of sin, or cycle of poverty, or maybe you are just familiar with a the spin cycle on the washing machine. I'd like to introduce you to the cycle of prayer. This illustrates the relationship between prayer and faith, and how it works:

First, we need to pray with at least a little bit of faith. Hebrews 11:6 says, "Without faith it is impossible to please God." And Jesus pointed out in Matthew 21:22 that "if you **believe**, you will receive **whatever** you ask for in prayer." So our initial prayer needs to have some faith.

Step 1.

PRAY IN FAITH

5   Billy Graham Evangelistic Association. 2009. "Notable Quotes from Billy Graham." Stories. November 30, 2018. https://billygraham.org/story/notable-quotes-from-billy-graham/

Step 2. As you pray, you will see God answer your prayer.

Step 3. The good news is that once you see God answer your prayer, your faith will naturally increase.

Since your faith has increased, the next time you go to God with a request, you will tend to pray with greater faith, boldness and fervency, right? You've seen him come through for you, so now you are inspired to pray at another level.

Step 4.

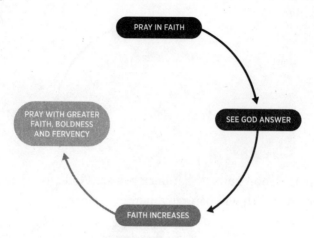

And, of course, as you pray with greater faith, boldness and fervency, you are more likely to see God answer your prayer, and the cycle of prayer is engaged.

Step 5. Completed Cycle

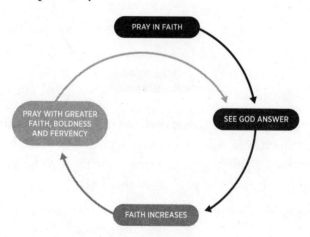

So, the key to kick-starting this cycle of prayer is . . . seeing God answer your prayers.

I earlier mentioned E.M. Bounds, a chaplain in the 1800s,

who wrote a series of small books on the subject of prayer that I would highly recommend. In his book *Possibilities of Prayer*, Bounds wrote, "It is answered prayer which brings prayer out of the realm of dry, dead things, and makes praying a thing of life and power."[6]

So how do we get answered prayer? Let's look at three principles of asking from God's Word.

3 Principles of Asking

1. Ask

To begin with, we obviously need to ask. Jesus said in John 14:13-14, "And I will do **whatever** you ask in my name, so that the Father may be glorified in the Son. You may ask me for **anything** in my name, and I will do it."

In Matthew 7:7-8, he explained,

> Ask and it will be given to you; seek and you will find; knock and the door will be opened to you. For everyone who asks receives; the one who seeks finds; and to the one who knocks, the door will be opened.

Did you notice that Jesus repeats this idea six times? You can't receive, find, or have it opened until you ask, seek, and knock.

2. Ask with Expectancy

If we pray without faith, James promises that we can expect to receive nothing! Encouraging us to pray for wisdom in James 1:6-8, he says:

> But when you ask, you must believe and not doubt, because the one who doubts is like a wave of the sea, blown and

---

6   Bounds, E.M. 2016. The *Complete Works of EM Bounds*. Dancing Unicorn Books. Kindle edition, location 7001

tossed by the wind. **That person should not expect to receive anything** from the Lord. Such a person is double-minded and unstable in all they do.

I must confess that I am sometimes guilty of praying without expecting God to answer. I just go through the motions of praying, not because I really want God to answer, but rather, it's just something that I am supposed to do.

E.M. Bounds had some interesting thoughts on this. He says in *The Possibilities of Prayer:*

> Not to be concerned about the answer to prayer is not to pray . . . What myriads of prayers have been offered for which no answer is returned, no answer longed for, and no answer expected! Conscious that God does not or has not answered us directly, we have [comforted] ourselves with the [wrong notion] that God has in some intangible way, and with unknown results, given us something better. Or we have comforted and nurtured our spiritual sloth by saying that it is not God's will to give it to us.[7]

Ouch! Unexpectant prayers can actually reverse the cycle of prayer. When we don't see answers, our prayers become less fervent, faithless, and half-hearted, resulting in more unanswered prayers.

Now, let me stop here and point out that God is not a vending machine. He is still the sovereign God, who decides how and when he will answer our prayers. Also, there are always reasons why God may not answer our prayers. Perhaps there is unconfessed sin in our lives, or our hearts are not aligned with his. Sometimes, God wants to teach us something. And sometimes, our prayers are simply not God's will. While there are many reasons why God chooses to not answer prayers, the focus of this chapter is to learn and apply the principles that will lead

---

7   Bounds, E.M. 2016. The *Complete Works of EM Bounds.* Dancing Unicorn Books. Kindle edition, location 7044

us to seeing God answer more of our prayers. So then, how else do we get answered prayers?

3. Be Specific in Your Ask

Let's look at the story about a blind beggar named Bartimaeus found in Mark 10:46-48.

> Then they came to Jericho. As Jesus and his disciples, together with a large crowd, were leaving the city, a blind man, Bartimaeus (which means "son of Timaeus"), was sitting by the roadside begging. When he heard that it was Jesus of Nazareth, he began to shout, "Jesus, Son of David, have mercy on me!" Many rebuked him and told him to be quiet, but he shouted all the more, "Son of David, have mercy on me!"

Now, at this point in the story, what, exactly is Bartimaeus asking for? When you get down to it, not much. He's asked for mercy, but what does that mean exactly? Maybe Jesus already showed him mercy by stopping and talking with him. His request is passionate, but vague.

> Jesus stopped and said, "Call him." So they called to the blind man, "Cheer up! On your feet! He's calling you." Throwing his cloak aside, he jumped to his feet and came to Jesus.

Now, notice at Jesus' response in verse 51:

> **"What do you want me to do for you?"** Jesus asked him.
> The blind man said, "Rabbi, I want to see."
> "Go," said Jesus, "your faith has healed you."
> Immediately he received his sight and followed Jesus along the road.

How do you think Bartimaeus' prayer life was, following this experience? Bartimaeus made his request —he wanted sight!— and Jesus answered it. As Jesus answered his prayer, it is safe to say that Bartimaeus' faith increased. And, as a result of that, I imagine his prayers became much more faith-filled, bold and passionate.

Andrew Murray, in his great classic, *With Christ in the School of Prayer,* said:

> So much of our prayer is vague and pointless. Some cry for mercy, but do not take the trouble to know exactly why they want it. Others ask to be delivered from sin, but do not name any sin from which deliverance can be claimed. Still others pray for God's blessing on those around them—for the outpouring of God's Spirit on their land or on the world— and yet have no special field where they can wait and expect to see the answer. And to everyone the Lord says, "What do you really want, and what do you expect me to do?"[8]

I believe that the key to answered prayers is to make **specific** requests so that we can clearly see God's answer to our prayers. When we see these specific requests answered, we glorify God, because it is so obvious that it was from him! In the next pages, I will share how God took me through this cycle several times while I was in university.

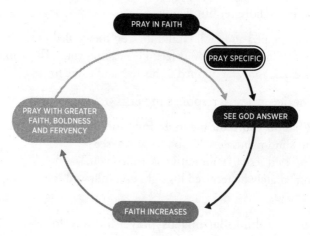

8   Murray, Andrew. 1981. *With Christ in the School of Prayer.* Springdale: Whitaker House. 75

Getting My Training Wheels at Baylor

During my first year at Baylor University, some friends and I started a ministry in the government housing projects next to campus. This was a poor and sometimes dangerous area, and we hoped to bring the gospel to this neighborhood. I must admit, we didn't really have any idea what we were doing, but we just kind of stepped out in faith, meeting the local kids and playing sports with them.

During this time, I had a prayer partner named Bret Franzen. He and I prayed each week about the things going on in our lives, and he asked me to consider some specific prayer requests related to this ministry. I said that I was enjoying spending time with these kids, but really wanted to see one kid come to faith. So we prayed for God to allow us to see one kid come to faith from the projects. Within ten days of that prayer, I saw three kids pray to receive Christ!

I prayed specifically.

I saw God answer.

My faith increased.

I prayed with greater faith, boldness and fervency.

Next, I recognized that I needed some help with this work. The friends who had originally started this felt that God was leading them a different direction, so I was pretty much on my own. I told Bret that I wanted to ask God for three people to help me, but that I did not want to ask them. I wanted them to come to me. In my mind, I was hoping for two women and a guy to come help me, so we could be more effective reaching both the boys and the girls in the area. Within the next week, I had two women and a guy independently approach me to ask if they could help.

I prayed specifically.

I saw God answer.

My faith increased.

I prayed with greater faith, boldness and fervency.

I decided to ask God to allow us to see one older teen and one adult place their trust in Christ before Christmas. In the weeks leading up to Christmas, I saw two older teens and one adult pray with me to receive Christ.

I prayed specifically.

I saw God answer.

My faith increased.

I prayed with greater faith, boldness and fervency.

The following fall, I decided to ask God for eight students to help me with this ministry. The ministry was continuing to grow, and I wanted to bring other people in to help me run it. God provided eight students to help me.

I prayed specifically.

I saw God answer.

My faith increased.

I prayed with greater faith, boldness and fervency.

As I was considering my summer plans, I recognized that if I was going to have a more lasting impact on these kids, I needed to stick around for the entire summer. So I prayed that God would provide me a job that would allow me to stay in Waco (where Baylor is located), make some money, and work in the projects.

Around that time, a friend introduced me to Jimmy Dorrell, a pastor of a small church in Waco. Jimmy told me that they had a desire to impact the disadvantaged of the city, and were looking to hire a summer intern to help run their ministry to inner city kids. Essentially, he said, he wanted to hire me to continue to do my work in partnership with his church. Unbelievable!

Sometime after that summer, a friend suggested that my specific prayers could be limiting God. Why ask for two people to trust Christ when maybe he wanted 100? Well, I didn't want to limit God, so I stopped praying specifically. And over the next two years, I cannot remember a single answered prayer.

During my last year at Baylor, I felt God calling me to join staff with Cru. One unique challenge of this job is that the staff are required to raise their personal support. My goal, at the time, was to raise $1500/month. That seemed like a huge goal! But that July, I was given some training and I determined to trust God and work really hard to complete it. I learned from my new staff team at the University of Georgia that there was a fall retreat happening on October 13. I told my team that that was my goal. They all smiled politely, patted me on the head, and basically said, "We'll see you in January," which was the time that most of our new staff tended to complete their personal support and report to campus.

As I began my support raising, I prayed fervently that God would allow me to complete my support and arrive at the University of Georgia by the fall retreat. And guess what? I arrived at the University of Georgia on October 12, with my support fully raised.

Praying For Friends

During this same time, I had been praying for a few friends of mine to come to faith. God had burdened my heart for Charles, Juan, Junior, and Mark to come to faith. These were friends from high school who had figured prominently in my life, and I wanted them to come to know Jesus. But, to be honest, after a while I stopped praying for them.

In the summer of 1991, I was on a summer missions project in San Diego, California. While I was there, I was talking with one of the staff who had happened to go to school at the same university as my friend, Charles.

She said, "I have a friend who plays football for our
university."

I said, "I also have a friend who plays football there."

She said, "My friend is a really strong Christian."

I said, "My friend is a real party animal. By the way, what is
your friend's name?"

"Charles Hampton."

"Charles is a Christian?!"

I couldn't believe it. So right then, I started praying for Juan,
Junior and Mark, and I continue to pray for them.

Praying For Campus Goals

During my last year at the University of Georgia, I shared this
principle of praying specifically with our students. Like many
campus ministries, we had a regular prayer time for our campus.
Following my challenge for us to pray specifically, the head of
our prayer ministry approached me and shared three goals for
which they were going to pray:

- For the size of the prayer meetings to double
- For 60 participants to go to a conference for fraternity and
  sorority students
- For 25 students to go on summer missions from the
  University of Georgia.

When they told me these goals, my first thought was: "Oh no!
These are ridiculous goals! There is no way we will see these
happen!" What a great man of faith I was! You see, at the time,
our "Greek" ministry (to fraternities and sororities) only had
a small handful of students involved. If you know anything
about the party life in the Greek system, you know that it has
not traditionally been a hotbed of spiritual passion. And yet this
small group wanted to invite 60 students from the Greek system
to attend a Christian conference for a weekend.

I thought these goals were really over the top, but because

I had just stood up in front of 250 students and told them to pray this way, I put on my best face, and joined the students in praying passionately for 60 students to attend this conference.

Over the next few weeks, our prayer movement grew, though I am not sure it doubled. But, as we approached the date of the Greek conference, it looked like God was doing a miracle. Slowly, students began to register, and on the day that the conference was to begin, the 59th and 60th students registered for the conference. God had answered our prayers!!

And do you want to guess how many students went on summer projects from the University of Georgia that year? That's right! Twenty-five.

Praying For Everything

The Apostle Paul writes in Philippians 4:6 NASB, "Be anxious for nothing, but in **everything** by prayer and supplication with thanksgiving **let your requests be made known to God.**"

For some reason, even though God is all-knowing, he commands us to let our requests be made known to him. This is more for our benefit than his. He wants us to acknowledge our need and to say it to him, so that when he does answer, we can see the connection, and give him the glory. And, frankly, I think God wants us to pray for all sorts of things. Not just the "big" things. Let me give you some examples.

In my times alone with God, I like to use a prayer journal (I'll explain more about this later). Journaling keeps me focused during my prayer time, and allows me to write down a lot of different things that I can pray for.

I've prayed for a cottage to be provided for our family to stay in for free. God provided that. I've prayed for a specific weight-loss goal. After years of praying, I finally saw it happen. I pray for a specific percentage return on my investments. Still not always seeing this one answered the way I want it! Several years ago, I prayed that God would provide a specific price for the home we were selling. We got it! I also prayed for specific features in the house we were buying—a fireplace and soaker tub—we got 'em! I also often pray for specific revenue goals for some of my friends' businesses.

As you can see, we can pray for everything! God does not always give me every single thing that I ask for (no good father does that), but I have found that as I have prayed specifically for many things, God has given me many of these things.

Praying God-sized Prayers

Praying specifically will allow us to clearly see God answer our prayers, resulting in greater faith. But I want to encourage you to take your prayers to the next level. If we really want to be a used by God to have a massive impact, then we need to pray huge, God-sized prayers. Let me explain.

Most Christians pray for God to meet their basic needs. We pray to do well on exams, to find a good parking space, heal us from our colds, etc. But let me paint you a picture.

Let's say that you are good friends with Bill Gates, who, as of this writing, is worth $88 billion. And let's say that Bill—because he really likes you—decides to make you an incredible offer. He says, "As you know, I have been giving away a lot of my wealth. And since you are a good friend of mine, I'd really like to give some of this to you. In fact, I would like to offer you up to $10 billion.

"Now, I don't want to force you to take all of this money, so I am only going to give you the amount of money you ask to receive. On this legal document, which I have signed, I have a blank space for you to write in the amount of money you would like to accept from me. If you write $10 billion, I will give you

$10 billion. If you write any number below that, I will give you that amount. It is entirely up to you!"

Blown away, you thank him for his incredibly generous offer. Your mind is spinning as you consider what you should accept. You don't want to appear greedy, and you start to feel a little bad. After all, if you take $10 billion, that will leave Bill with only $78 billion. So, you decide to be humble about it, and write an amount that seems right to you:

$200.

Smiling, you hand the paper back to Bill Gates, who then looks at you incredulously. He is stunned and a little offended that you asked for so little, when he offered you so much. He pulls out his wallet, peels off two $100 bills and turns away, shaking his head.

"Maybe I should have asked for more," you think.

This illustration seems ridiculous, but isn't it similar to the way we pray to God? God has offered us this incredible tool to accomplish his purposes, promising us that we can ask him for anything in Jesus' name. And yet, so many of our prayers are small and timid.

Let's take God at his Word! James 5:16 says, "The effective prayer of a righteous man can accomplish much." Luke 1:37 says, "For **nothing** will be impossible with God." And as we've already mentioned, Ephesians 3:20 says: "Now to him who is able to do exceeding, abundantly beyond what we are able to ask or think" (NASB 1977)

What would happen if our prayers reflected these truths about God?

Asking God For Big Things

While I was in my second year at Baylor University, a friend and I had a vision to see God do something significant through

Baylor students. So we took God at his Word and prayed for three huge things:

First, that God would begin a prayer movement at Baylor.

Second, that spiritual awakening would occur at Baylor.

And, third, that Baylor would be made one of the greatest sending grounds of Christian workers in the world.

In Matthew 9:37-38 NASB, Jesus says, "The harvest is plentiful, but the workers are few. Therefore beseech the Lord of the harvest to raise up laborers into His harvest."

In this verse, the Greek word for beseech is *"deomai."* Deomai is a strong word that means to beg or to plead for something. So here, Jesus is commanding his disciples to beg God to raise up laborers for the harvest. Do you know that this is the only time in Scripture that we are commanded to beg God for something? Seems like more laborers are pretty important to God. So, as students at Baylor, we obeyed that command and begged God that he would use our campus to become one of the greatest sending grounds of Christian workers in the world.

Over the next three years, several of us prayed consistently for these things. By my fourth year, I can confidently say that . . . we didn't see a lot.

We definitely saw an increase of prayer on our campus. I heard of prayer groups popping up all over the campus. Was it a prayer movement? Tough to say. It was a little hard to measure.

How about spiritual awakening? Well, certainly nothing like what I have read about, where thousands of people are coming to faith, believers are repenting of sin, and churches are overflowing. But we did see that there was a significant growth in people involved in ministries on campus. At one point, more than 10% of the campus was involved in some sort of a weekly Bible study or worship service on campus, which is pretty cool. I would not say that God granted spiritual awakening at Baylor at that time, though he was certainly sparking growth among believers there.

So, I share these to point out that just because we pray big, doesn't mean that God is obligated to answer our requests. But, I do think God answered that third request. Let me tell you what God did.

During my first year at Baylor, there were probably about 30 or so students who took part in summer missions. During my last year, there were well over 100 students who took part in short or long-term missions trips. Pretty cool!

A couple of years later, a friend and I were discussing Cru's "STINT" (Short Term International) program, which was a one-year missions trip somewhere overseas. "Do you know which campus has more students on STINT than any other campus in the world?" he asked.

"Baylor?" I hopefully replied.

"That's right!" he said. And we celebrated God beginning to answer our prayers.

A few years after that, I had moved to Canada, and was meeting with a church leader in St. John's, Newfoundland. I was helping to launch new campus ministries across Canada, and began a discussion with this leader about launching something in the easternmost province of Canada.

"If you want to reach university students, you need to read this," he said as he tossed me a book on small groups. I opened it up and saw that it was written by a guy named Jimmy Seibert. I knew Jimmy. Jimmy was a student at Baylor who had discipled my old prayer partner and discipler, Bret.

In the intro to the book, it explained that Jimmy's church had been involved in sending hundreds of students from his church in Waco on short-term missions trips. Most of these were Baylor students. I called the church to learn more, and was told that over the previous two years, they had sent groups of 250, then 350 students on short-term missions! Wow! God was answering our prayers!

A couple of years after that, during the summer of 1998, I

was on a six-week missions trip to Bangkok, Thailand, with our
ministry. Our students had spent a few weeks sharing the gospel
with university students in this unreached, Buddhist nation. I
was visiting our students on campus one day when I bumped
into some North American students. We started chatting, and
I discovered they were from Texas and were tied into Jimmy
Seibert's church.

"I went to school at Baylor!" I told them enthusiastically,
"and I was discipled by a guy who was discipled by Jimmy."

"What's his name?" they asked.

"Bret Franzen," I said.

"Bret is here!" they said. I couldn't believe it!

It was such a cool picture of how God had answered our
prayers. I was a Baylor grad working in Canada, involved in
mobilizing Canadian students to take the gospel to the nations.
Here I was sharing the gospel in Bangkok, Thailand on a
six-week missions trip. Bret later explained to me that he and
his wife were serving as missionaries in a nearby Asian nation
(which at the time was one of the least reached countries in the
world), trying to plant a church. He "just happened" to be in
Bangkok for a few days for a dentist appointment.

"Bret," I said, "do you remember how, during our first year at
Baylor, we used to pray that God would raise up laborers for the
harvest from Baylor? We are part of the answer to those prayers!"

I recently read another book by Jimmy Seibert, *Passion
and Purpose*. Jimmy continues to pastor his church in Waco,
Texas, that had sent out Bret and the missions team that was
in Thailand. But that church has multiplied, planting dozens of
churches all over the world. I was blown away to read that God
has, through that church, sent out thousands of people to take
the gospel all over the world. Many of those students were from
Baylor. God has answered our prayers!

A Young Student's Story

In 1997, I was speaking at a student retreat in Ontario. One of the young men there was named Sean. Sean was a skinny first-year student who was leader of a fledgling campus ministry at the University of Guelph. At the time, he was one of only six students who were involved in that ministry, which was exclusively student-run.

After hearing me tell this story about Baylor, Sean told me that he wanted to begin praying that God would use the University of Guelph to become one of the greatest sending grounds of Christian workers in the world. That year, those six students met regularly, asking God to send out laborers from their campus to the world. In the next several years, the ministry at Guelph grew to over 120 students. Students from that campus helped to launch new ministries at Wilfrid Laurier University, the University of Waterloo and McMaster University. In the next ten years, more than 75 students from those four campuses entered full-time ministry as laborers, including Sean and four others of those original six students. Since that time, I have seen similar fruit from several other Canadian campuses.

So what are you asking God for?

The picture I have of God is him waiting to pounce on our prayers. He loves it when we pray, and he loves it when he can show his glory by bringing about the answer to huge prayers that are aligned to his Word.

We need to pray specific prayers, but also visionary prayers:

- Pray that your campus or church or neighborhood becomes one of the greatest sending grounds of missionaries in all of the world.
- Ask God to allow dozens to come to faith through your personal ministry in your workplace, campus or community.

- Pray that spiritual awakening sweeps through your country as a direct result of your ministry.
- Pray that God allows our generation to see the fulfillment of the Great Commission. There is only one generation that will get to see the fulfillment of the Great Commission. Let's ask him that it be ours!

I love what Dawson Trotman, the founder of Navigators, said about prayer:

> When you say, "Father in heaven," you have addressed God the Father, the Maker of the universe, the One who holds the worlds in his hands. What did you ask for? Did you ask for peanuts, or toys? Or did you ask for continents?

Let's ask Jesus for continents!

So what happened with Gary, the guy I had been praying would give $100 million over his lifetime? It's a pretty cool story.

Around 2012, I had begun praying some really big prayers about how I would like to see God use me to impact the world for his Kingdom over my lifetime. So I began asking him for "ridiculous" requests like, "Use me to help reach 1000 unreached people groups" and "Allow me to impact millions of Muslims with the gospel." One of those crazy prayers was to allow me to be used to mobilize $1 billion for the Kingdom. Up to that point, the largest financial gift I had ever been a part of was for $75,000, and God had dropped that one in my lap. So while I knew that praying for $1 billion was a relatively "ridiculous" prayer, I committed to praying for it anyways.

Gary and I had been growing in our friendship and I knew that he had given some large, multi-million dollar gifts to universities, hospitals, etc. Wanting to learn how to raise large gifts like that, I decided to ask Gary's advice. In the months prior, I had been praying that Gary would give $100 million to Kingdom causes over his lifetime, but at this point, I simply wanted to do a thought exercise with him to grow in my ability to raise large donations.

"Gary, I want to make clear that I am not asking you for this money right now, but I see lots of multi-million dollar gifts that go towards things like hospitals, universities, and significant building projects. Those are all worthy investments, but you know as well as I do that the only thing that is ultimately going to change the world is evangelism and discipleship."

Gary eagerly agreed, and encouraged me to go on.

"However, I have rarely, if ever, seen a multi-million dollar gift for evangelism and discipleship. So, if you are willing, I would like to brainstorm with you about how this might look, to ask someone for, say, $5 million towards evangelism."

Gary sat up enthusiastically. "I really like this idea! What if. . ."

And so began our conversation. And in the course of our discussion, Gary expressed an interest in further exploring the idea of giving $5 million towards this vision. Wow!

A few weeks later, we met again, so I circled back to the discussion. "Gary, do you remember that discussion about the hypothetical $5 million gift for evangelism?"

"Yes! I really like that", he replied. "Let's continue to talk about it, but let's say it's $10 million."

"Why not?" I laughed. It was still hypothetical anyways.

A few weeks after that, Gary and I were having another lunch together, and continued to talk more about the idea of creating a foundation to manage this (hypothetical) gift. That's when he dropped the bomb.

"I really like this idea," he said, "and the timing is right for me to take some money out of my business, so I'd like to start a foundation focused on evangelism in the least reached parts of the world. And I am going to start it with $40 million."

I calmly nodded my head, thanked him for his incredible

generosity, and then excused myself to go to the bathroom where I completely freaked out!

"God, I am not smart enough or gifted enough to be part of something this huge!!" I was completely overwhelmed. But I composed myself and went back to our table, where Gary and I started working through a plan to make this a reality.

As I wrestled over this during the next several weeks, my emotions ping-ponged between elation and terror. But as I processed it and prayed about it further, God spoke to me, "I am not allowing you to be a part of this gift because you deserve it. I am mobilizing this money because I chose to. And besides, you were asking for this, weren't you?"

Several months later, as Gary and I worked on setting up the foundation, he dropped another bomb.

"My family said they want to pull some more money out of the business for various reasons, so I am going to be adding an additional $60 million to the foundation, for a total of $100 million."

This time, I just laughed. God had answered my prayer! In less than a year!

Today, Gary and I are working with some incredible leaders to give away this money to advance the gospel around the world. The focus of this foundation is to specifically fund evangelism, with a focus on works in the least evangelized parts of the world. I am humbled that God has allowed me to play a part in seeing this vision come to fruition and in helping to give away several million dollars a year towards helping to fulfill the Great Commission.

Now, all of a sudden, my "ridiculous" prayer for God to allow me to mobilize $1 billion is not that crazy. And this foundation will potentially allow me to impact millions of Muslims, and help bring the gospel of Jesus Christ to over 1000 unreached people groups. Incredible! I don't know if God will allow me to mobilize $1 billion, but I am 10% of the way there now. And today, Gary and I are praying for a few other very wealthy business folks we know to also invest over $500 million in Kingdom priorities. You want to join me in that?

Let's Get Practical

Seven Steps To Expand the Scope and Impact of Your Prayers

I want to remind you that I did not start out as a university student praying for $100 million. In fact, back then, I was asking God to provide $500 for my inner city ministry—and he did! Over the years, my faith has grown and so have my prayers. So let me take the next few pages to walk you through seven practical steps to help you expand the scope and impact of your prayers.

1. Keep A Prayer Journal

I have found my prayer journal tremendously helpful over the years. I find that a journal helps to keep me focused, as my mind can easily wander during my times of prayer. I also like that it allows me to write down and then remember lots of requests from friends and family. A lot of times people ask, "Will you pray for _____?" You enthusiastically agree to do that, and then promptly forget. Having a journal ensures that I can always record and pray for these requests.

I have also developed a simple system that has served me well. This is a guideline, and I by no means follow it every day, but it always provides me with clarity and direction in my prayers.

In my system, I number my requests one to four. Today I will pray for the "ones," tomorrow for the "twos," etc. This allows me to pray for more requests, as I don't have to get through

every request every day. It also allows me to keep my prayer
requests fresh, as I rotate through a different set of requests every
four days. That said, I have also included an "E" next to some
requests. These are things that I do want to pray for every day. I
might pray for an upcoming event, or for a friend who is facing
a particularly challenging health or personal issue. Below is an
example of how my prayer journal works:

1. Give me wisdom in juggling my multiple responsibilities
2. John Stevens – come to faith
3. Godfrey Asante – anoint his ministry in Tanzania
4. Help me raise $1.3 million for our ministries by July of
   2019
1. Allow me to recruit 10 leaders to take part in the
   November missions trip
2. Heal Stacey's cancer
3. Saudi royal family – allow several to come to faith
4. Let Jim Robertson introduce two employees to faith by
   December 2020
1. Allow me to have 10 men join my small group
E. Thank God for something
2. Randy and Susan: neighbours – come to faith
3. Give Sheila wisdom on career direction
E. Help David Jones get a job by the end of April
4. Allow me to mobilize $1 billion for your Kingdom over my
   lifetime
1. Allow 75 students from Queen's University to attend our
   fall retreat
2. Let Bob Lee's company generate $2 million by the end of
   the year
3. Help me reflect Jesus better with my family
4. Ben Josephson's church plant grow to 50 people by end of
   this year.
E. Give my kids wisdom in school and career choices.

As you can see, I have a wide range of things that I pray for. To encourage me and keep me motivated, when I see an answer to prayer, I will write "thanks" next to the item. This allows me to refer back to my many answered prayers over the years, which helps strengthen my faith.

Also, sometimes, after praying for something for a long time, I will cross it off of my list. I must confess that I can grow bored praying for some people or things after a while (a prayer warrior, I ain't!), but by crossing things off my list, I can add lots of new things to the list. For example, I have prayed off and on for Saudi Arabia, and more specifically, Mecca, for years. I will cross it off and then a few months later add it again. I will pray for Juan, Mark, Junior and Charles on occasion, but sometimes I drop them from my list for a while. Doing this also ensures that my list is not overwhelmingly long.

Sometimes, God simply says "no" to my prayer requests. In those instances, I thank God for his wisdom and sovereignty and begin praying for something else. It can be disappointing, but it is helpful to focus on God's character and trust that his plans are better than mine.

This system has helped me stay relatively consistent in my times of prayer over the years, but I also try to mix things up so that my prayer times are fresh. Some days I simply listen to worship music. I will take prayer walks. I will often pray while I am driving (with my eyes open!), or waiting in line, or when I'm having trouble sleeping. I also try to take a personal retreat every year where I spend extended time in prayer. My prayer journal is simply a tool that has been helpful for me, so you may want to try it as well.

2. Pray Specific Prayers

Let me encourage you to pray specific, measurable, answerable prayer requests. This will increase the likelihood that you will be able to see God answer your prayers. Ask God about some specific goals or ideas to pray for, and then add them to your list. I did not start out asking God for $1 billion. I started out with much smaller requests, and as God answered hundreds of my prayers over my lifetime, my faith grew to the point where I could ask him for much more.

3. Find a Prayer Partner

Get a prayer partner or partners and pray for each other weekly. This will force you to be specific, and will encourage you to keep praying.

4. Be Audience Specific

Pray with your primary audience, in your primary audience, for your primary audience. Here is what I mean. When I was at the University of Georgia, I led a Bible study with guys who all lived in Russell Residence. Every week, we met in that residence and prayed for the people of that residence. We prayed for friends who did not know Jesus. We prayed for the Christians to stay strong and reach out. We prayed for the leaders of the building. And we asked God to raise up laborers for the harvest. Over the years, we saw God grow the ministry in that residence, and we can point to several laborers in ministry who came through that dorm!

Similarly, you can pray for the same types of things in your workplace, or your neighborhood. Pull together some co-workers and meet in a boardroom before or after hours to pray for the people in your office. Or take prayer walks around your neighborhood with some others from your church. You don't need to make a show of anything, but it can be helpful to build regular times to ask God to open hearts to his gospel.

5. Commit to Corporate Prayer

If your campus or church or workplace has a regular prayer time, commit to joining it at least every other week. If there is not one, start one. Many people prefer meeting first thing in the morning, as there are rarely scheduling conflicts, but it can be just as valuable to meet in the middle of the day for 20 minutes. Our U of Georgia prayer meeting was Friday mornings, and our Russell Residence prayer time was 2:30 p.m. on Wednesdays.

6. Ask God to Give You a Great Vision for What to Trust Him For

Acknowledge to God that you cannot dream big on your own, but that you need him to give you that God-sized vision. I believe God will honor your humility and dependence and give you something that is exciting!

7. Become a Prayer Mobilizer

If you want to have an even bigger impact, become a prayer mobilizer. I have been inspired by this quote from Leonard Ravenhill:

> The man (or woman) who could get believers to praying would, under God, usher in the greatest revival that the world has ever known.[9]

BE THAT PERSON!!! Ask God to use you as a catalyst for his people to become praying people.

Prayer is an incredible gift from our all-loving, all-powerful God. Let's use it! Pray specifically, so we can glorify God when he answers specifically, and pray God-sized prayers, so he is glorified when he does exceeding abundantly beyond all we ask or imagine!

---

9 Christian Quotes. 2017. Leonard Ravenhill Quotes. Accessed Feb 5, 2019. http://www.quoteschristian.com/leonardravenhill.html

CHAPTER 4

Think Eternally, Live Accordingly

In Genesis, chapters two and three tell the story of the creation and the fall of Adam and Eve. The beauty of chapter two is shattered by the tragedy of chapter three, which describes how Adam and Eve's perfect fellowship with God was broken. However, in the middle of this sad narrative, there are two beautiful pictures of grace. Let me recount the story.

Genesis 2:15-17 says,

> The Lord God took the man and put him in the Garden of Eden to work it and take care of it. And the Lord God commanded the man, "You are free to eat from any tree in the garden; but you must not eat from the tree of the knowledge of good and evil, for when you eat of it you will surely die."

That sounds pretty clear, doesn't it? You can eat from any tree in creation, except one. This is not a complex or confusing command. Just "don't eat from that one tree."

Of course, we know the story. Adam and Eve ate the fruit from the tree of knowledge of good and evil. When they ate that fruit, they died spiritually—their relationship with God was broken—and they began to die physically—all because of their sin. Their new reality was to live the rest of their physical lives with a fallen, sinful nature.

In Genesis 3:14-20, God explains the various consequences of their actions. From this point forward, Eve will experience painful childbirth and broken relationship with her husband. For Adam, he could expect painful toil and suffering throughout his life.

I'd read this account many times, but one day I was struck

by God's act of grace in Genesis 3:21 immediately following the explanation of these consequences. It says, "The LORD God made garments of skin for Adam and his wife and clothed them." Wow! Adam and Eve had rebelled, and as a result, they were now living with the shame of their nakedness before God. So how did God respond?

He didn't mock them.

He didn't rage at their self-reliance.

He didn't tell them that they deserved this shame.

Instead, God shows them grace. He covers their shame by killing an animal and using its skin to make clothes for Adam and Eve. This would be the first of many animals that would die as a substitute for mankind's sin. I can picture God lovingly and patiently explaining to them, "This is how you make clothing. You haven't needed this before, but I created these animals to help meet your needs."

That is not the response I would expect from an angry God!

But as we keep reading in Genesis 3:22-24, an even bigger demonstration of God's grace is revealed:

> And the Lord God said, "The man has now become like one of us, knowing good and evil. He must not be allowed to reach out his hand and take also from the tree of life and eat, and live forever." **So** the Lord God banished him from the Garden of Eden to work the ground from which he had been taken. After he drove the man out, he placed on the east side of the Garden of Eden cherubim and a flaming sword flashing back and forth to guard the way to the tree of life.

You may have never thought of Adam and Eve's banishment from Eden as an act of grace. But the Word says that God did not want Adam and Eve to eat from the tree of life, **so**, he removed them from the Garden of Eden. If God was going to allow people to live forever, he did not want their eternal lives to be lived in this sin-stained, pain-filled, guilt-ridden, violent and hateful world. He had a much better plan for our eternal dwelling. God will give his people another opportunity to eat from the tree of life, and to live forever, but this time it will be in heaven, where we will live with Christ-like, sin-free bodies.

Living For Eternity

When we speak of living forever, I think that most of us have a hard time comprehending what that means. So let me try to give you an illustration.

You and I will probably live for between 80-100 years. So, to begin to get a grasp on eternity, let me try to paint a picture that is, admittedly, insufficient. In the diagram below, you can see that our lives are represented by a very short space representing 100 years at the beginning of the line. The line, which seems to go on forever, represents the first day in heaven. And, as you know, we will live for millions of "heaven days."

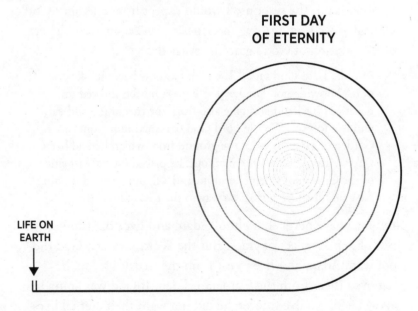

So, knowing that we will spend, *at most*, 100 years in this life-time, and that we will spend, *at least*, millions of years in heaven, how should we live our lives? I would recommend that we adopt this habit: think eternally, and live accordingly.

A Glimpse At Eternity

Our life on this planet is a fleeting stopover on our way to an eternal existence. And since we are going to live for billions of years after this life, it would make sense that we view our lives through the lens of eternity.

I will spend the bulk of this chapter focusing on heaven and the accompanying rewards. But I would not be representing the biblical view of eternity accurately or responsibly if I did not discuss the reality of hell. So let's address that first.

God's Judgement

Hebrews 9:27 NASB says, "It is appointed for men to die once and after this comes judgment."

The Apostle John, in I John 5:11-13, clearly explains the basis of our judgement:

> And this is the testimony: God has given us eternal life, and this life is in his Son. Whoever has the Son has life; whoever does not have the Son of God does not have life. I write these things to you who believe in the name of the Son of God so that you may know that you have eternal life.

For those of us who have received Jesus' gift of salvation by faith—asked him to forgive our sins and take control of our lives—we can be assured that our salvation is secure, based on what Jesus did for us on the cross. For those who have not, John explains the consequences in Revelation 20:15, "Anyone whose name was not found written in the book of life was thrown into the lake of fire."

Hell, obviously, is not a very popular subject, and I really

don't like talking about it. But we cannot dismiss it, because
the Bible speaks of it often, and Jesus himself spoke about it on
multiple occasions.

During the Sermon on the Mount, in Matthew 5:29, Jesus
says, "If your right eye causes you to stumble, gouge it out and
throw it away. It is better for you to lose one part of your body
than for your whole body to be thrown into hell."

Later, in Matthew 10:28, Jesus said, "Do not be afraid of
those who kill the body but cannot kill the soul. Rather, be
afraid of the One who can destroy both soul and body in hell."

And in Matthew 25:41, when describing the separation of
the sheep from the goats, he says, "Then he [God] will say to
those on his left, 'Depart from me, you who are cursed, into the
eternal fire prepared for the devil and his angels.'"

I have to admit that when I read these words of Jesus, a chill
runs down my spine. I hate thinking about hell. But since Jesus
spoke about hell as a real place, we must assume that hell is real.
When Jesus spoke about it, he wasn't using a "scare tactic." He
was simply issuing a warning about a terrifying reality for all
who have sinned and who have rejected his free gift. This is the
same as someone who flags down motorists during a nighttime
rainstorm to warn them about a washed out bridge ahead. The
intent is not to frighten, it is simply alerting them to a real
danger ahead.

Hell will not be a place where people party together with
their buddies, as so many people like to think. Instead, Jesus
says that "in that place, there will be weeping and gnashing of
teeth" (Luke 13:28 NASB).

Paul describes how one day Jesus will "punish those who do
not know God and do not obey the gospel of our Lord Jesus.
They will be punished with everlasting destruction and shut out
from the presence of the Lord and from the glory of his might"
(II Thessalonians 1:8-9).

Like I said, I don't like even thinking about hell. But it

is important that I consider the possibility that many of the people I know and love could be on their way to hell. The good news is that it doesn't have to be that way. Peter explains in II Peter 3:9, "The Lord is not slow in keeping his promise, as some understand slowness. Instead he is patient with you, not wanting anyone to perish, but everyone to come to repentance."

The good news is that when people do repent, and give their hearts and lives to Jesus, hell is depopulated, and heaven's citizenship rolls are increased.

What Will Heaven Be Like?

I am so excited to get to heaven! Heaven is going to be incredible! I Corinthians 2:9 NLT says, "No eye has seen, nor ear heard, nor the heart of man imagined, what God has prepared for those who love him."

I find it incredible that the God who created the universe, and who sent his Son to die for us, has also been preparing an incredible homecoming for those of us who are in Christ.

While we cannot fully comprehend what we will see and experience in heaven right now, there are a few clues about heaven that Scripture has given us to tantalize us about what is to come. Let me try to explain some of what we will see and experience in heaven, based on what has been revealed in Scripture.

We're Home!

In my job, I do a lot of travelling. While I do enjoy most trips, I have to admit that my favorite part is usually at the end, when I walk in the front door of my house, and set my suitcase down. I am home. There is such a sense of comfort and peace knowing that I am back in the familiarity of my own home.

I think we will experience a similar sensation upon our arrival in heaven. Paul said in II Corinthians 5:6-8,

Therefore we are always confident and know that as long as we are at home in the body we are away from the Lord. For we live by faith, not by sight. We are confident, I say, and would prefer to be away from the body and at home with the Lord.

In Revelation 21:3, John writes that this feeling will be confirmed by a pronouncement:

And I heard a loud voice from the throne saying, "Look! God's dwelling place is now among the people, and he will dwell with them. They will be his people, and God himself will be with them and be their God."

New Bodies!

There is something else that I am really looking forward to upon our arrival in heaven—our new, Christ-like, sinless bodies! Paul says in Philippians 3:20-21,

Our citizenship is in heaven. And we eagerly await a Savior from there, the Lord Jesus Christ, who, by the power that enables him to bring everything under his control, will **transform our lowly bodies so that they will be like his glorious body.**

I don't know about you, but I am particularly excited about getting this new, glorious body. You may look good now, but it ain't nothing compared to what your new glorified body will look like! And we will no longer have to deal with the regular assault of aches, pains or diseases that we have to endure on this planet.

New Surroundings!

But it is not only our bodies that will be beautiful—heaven itself will be stunningly gorgeous! During my travels, I have spent time in places like the Caribbean and South Pacific, the Rocky Mountains, the plains of Africa, and many other beautiful places on earth. But these will all pale when compared to the beauty of heaven, because these places, though beautiful, exist in a fallen world. Do you remember Jesus' words to the thief on the cross next to him at his crucifixion in Luke 23:43? "Truly I tell you, today you will be with me in **paradise**."

In the book of Revelation, the Apostle John does his best to describe his time in heaven. As he writes, and tries to describe what he sees, he finds himself overwhelmed, and uses the most colorfully descriptive words he can come up with:

> "A rainbow that shone like an emerald encircled the throne" (Revelation 4:3).
> "From the throne came flashes of lightning, rumblings and peals of thunder" (Revelation 4:5).
> "His eyes were like blazing fire. His feet were like bronze glowing in a furnace, and his voice was like the sound of rushing waters" (Revelation 1:14-15).

Talk about sensory overload! And when John tried to describe the new city we will be inhabiting, he uses the metaphor of one of the most beautiful images he could think of—a gorgeous bride. "I saw the Holy City, the new Jerusalem, coming down out of heaven from God, prepared as a bride beautifully dressed for her husband" (Revelation 21:2).

Is there anything more beautiful than a bride beautifully dressed for her husband? This place is spectacular!"

Meeting Jesus!

The thing that I most look forward to in heaven, however, is meeting Jesus face to face! I picture your initial encounter with Jesus like this: You will fall on your face in awe-struck amazement. But before you can say anything, he will sweep you up into his arms and engulf you with a love-filled embrace. He will be beaming with joy as he looks directly into your eyes and says, "I have been waiting for you and am so excited to lavish my love upon you from now into eternity!!"

Incredible Joy!

Now that you are with Jesus, you will find yourself completely overwhelmed with a deep joy that saturates your entire being. And at that point, you will understand what David meant when he writes in Psalm 16:11 NASB, "In Your presence is fullness of joy; In Your right hand there are pleasures forever."

This joy that we will experience will be so complete and all-consuming that it will totally engulf any sadness or pain we have felt before. We are told in Revelation 21:4 that "he will wipe every tear from their eyes. There will be no more death or mourning or crying or pain, for the old order of things has passed away."

The Tree of Life - Redux

Remember how God removed Adam and Eve from Eden, so that they wouldn't live forever on earth? Well, once we are in heaven in our new glorified bodies and abiding daily with Jesus, the access to this life-giving tree will be restored, allowing us to live forever in paradise.

"Whoever has ears, let them hear what the Spirit says to the churches. To the one who is victorious, I will give the right to eat from the tree of life, which is in the **paradise** of God." Revelation 2:7

Are you beginning to get excited about going to heaven? But wait! There's more!

Eternal Rewards

All of the things I just described are promised to every Christ-follower. And if that were all there were, it would be incredibly awesome! But God has even more in store for you: eternal rewards!

In II Timothy 4:7-8, Paul says:

> I have fought the good fight, I have finished the race, I have kept the faith. Now there is in store for me the **crown of righteousness,** which the Lord, the righteous Judge, will **award** to me on that day—and not only to me, but also to all who have longed for his appearing.

The Bible speaks of rewards several other times as well.

> If anyone builds on this foundation using gold, silver, costly stones, wood, hay or straw, their work will be shown for what it is, because the Day will bring it to light. It will be revealed with fire, and the fire will test the quality of each person's work. If what has been built survives, the builder will receive a **reward** (I Corinthians 3:12-14).
>
> Do you not know that in a race all the runners run, but only one gets the prize? Run in such a way as to get the prize. Everyone who competes in the games goes into strict training. They do it to get a crown that will not last; but **we do it to get a crown that will last forever.** Therefore I do not run like someone running aimlessly; I do not fight like a boxer beating the air (I Corinthians 9:24-26).
>
> Serve wholeheartedly, as if you were serving the Lord, not people, because you know that the Lord will **reward** each one for whatever good they do, whether they are slave or free (Ephesians 6:7-8).

Our salvation is a free gift, obtained by grace through faith (Ephesians 2:8-9). However, our rewards are earned. During the remainder of this chapter, I would like to share some thoughts on how to maximize your eternal rewards.

Invest in Things that will Last for Eternity

Several years ago, I was given some shares of stock in a fast-growing and well-respected company (I'll call it Company A). In 1998, I held about $20,000 worth of this stock, which made me feel rich! But over the next two years, this stock, which was listed in the top 50 of the Fortune 500, tripled in value, expanding my holdings to over $60,000! The company was glowingly referenced in numerous books and investment magazines, and was about as safe an investment as you could want.

About the same time, there was another company that was doing quite well, but seemed like a much riskier investment. This company (Company B) was a tech start-up that seemed to have a bright future, but there was no track record, so it was hard to predict its future. But if it could stay in business and achieve its goals, there was potential for significant profit. With the right connections, I could have potentially invested my $20,000 in this company. But because I preferred to invest in something that I could see vs. some unseen potential, I left my money with Company A and didn't even try to invest in Company B.

The real name of Company A? Enron. Enron, you may have heard, was one of the most respected companies in the US. But near the end of year 2000, accounting irregularities were discovered, and soon it was revealed that much of the company's profits were fake. Enron's leaders had been lying to shareholders, the Securities Exchange Commission, and even to friends and business partners. In a very short time, this high-flying company was exposed as a complete fraud. In a matter of months, the share price plunged from $90/share to pennies a share, and then became completely worthless. Because of the speed with which this happened, and because of my inexperience as an investor, I was only able to recover about $1,500 of the $60,000 that I had held just a few weeks before then. It was devastating. So what happened to Company B?

The real name of Company B is Google. Perhaps you've heard of them. If I had taken out just 10% of my Enron holdings in 1998 and invested that money in Google stock, my $2,000 would, as of the time of this writing, be worth over $96 million!

While that is a depressing story (especially for me!), let me add a hypothetical wrinkle to this story. Let's say that in the year 1998, I was given access to a time machine, which allowed me to jump ahead 20 years. In this scenario, when I was transported to the year 2018, I would look at the stock history of both Enron and Google. I would see that the management of Enron had been convicted of fraud and was in prison, and that the company itself was completely worthless. At the same time, I would see that Google had become one of the most valuable companies on earth. I could then have jumped in my time machine, gone back to 1998, and invested my money according to that information.

Now let's say that, possessing that knowledge, I decided to not do anything differently in 1998. Knowing the future of both of these companies, I still chose to leave all of my money in Enron, and pass up the opportunity to invest in Google before anyone had heard of it. Can we agree that that would have been incredibly stupid?

If I knew the future of these two investments with certainty, my only rational action would be to sell everything I possessed (especially investments that would be worthless in 20 years) and invest in the company that would have incredible returns on my investment.

Great Eternal Investment Advice

We actually have an investment advisor who doesn't need a time machine, because he transcends time, past, present and future.

He knows and controls the future, and has provided some "insider tips" to allow us to have an incredible return on our earthly investments. Let me share a few of these insider tips from Jesus and some of his followers:

Jesus
>The kingdom of heaven is like treasure hidden in a field.
>When a man found it, he hid it again, and then in his joy
>went and sold all he had and bought that field. Again, the
>kingdom of heaven is like a merchant in search of fine pearls.
>When he found one of great value, he went away and sold
>everything he had and bought it (Matthew 13:44-46).
>Do not store up for yourselves treasures on earth, where
>moths and vermin destroy, and where thieves break in and
>steal. But store up for yourselves treasures in heaven, where
>moths and vermin do not destroy, and where thieves do not
>break in and steal. For where your treasure is, there your heart
>will be also (Matthew 6:19-21).

Paul
>So we fix our eyes not on what is seen, but on what is unseen,
>since what is seen is temporary, but what is unseen is eternal
>(II Corinthians 4:18).

Peter
>But the day of the Lord will come like a thief. The heavens
>will disappear with a roar; the elements will be destroyed by
>fire, and the earth and everything done in it will be laid bare.
>Since everything will be destroyed in this way, what kind of
>people ought you to be? You ought to live holy and godly
>lives as you look forward to the day of God and speed its
>coming (II Peter 3:10-12).

Thomas à Kempis
>"Let temporal things serve your use, but the eternal be the
>object of your desire."[1]

1   Alcorn, Randy. 1999. *In Light of Eternity: Perspectives on Heaven*. Colorado:Waterbrook Press. Pg 14

John Wesley

"I judge all things only by the price they shall gain in eternity."[2]

C.S. Lewis

"If we consider the unblushing promises of reward and the staggering nature of the rewards promised in the Gospels, it would seem that our Lord finds our desires not too strong, but too weak. We are half-hearted creatures, fooling about with drink and sex and ambition when infinite joy is offered us, like an ignorant child who wants to go on making mud pies in a slum because he cannot imagine what is meant by the offer of a holiday at the sea. We are far too easily pleased."[3]

Jim Elliot

"He is no fool who gives up what he cannot keep to gain what he cannot lose."[4]

It is obvious that God wants us to live our lives in light of eternity. So how can we do that? Let me give you a few practical suggestions.

Let's Get Practical

Think Eternally

First, develop an eternal perspective. There are a few ways to do this:

- Take time, every once in a while, to stop and reflect on eternity. King David prayed for this in Psalm 39:4-5: "Show me, LORD, my life's end and the number of my days; let me know how fleeting my life is. You have made my days a mere handbreadth; the span of my years is as

2   Alcorn, Randy. 2003. *The Law of Rewards: Giving what you can't keep to gain what you can't lose.* Illinois: Tyndale House Publishers. Pg 18
3   Lewis, C.S. 1949. *The Weight of Glory: and other addresses.* New York: Harper Collins One, Harper Collins. Pgs 1-2
4   Elliot, Elisabeth. 2009. *Shadow of the Almighty.* New York: Harper Collins, pg 15

nothing before you. Everyone is but a breath, even those
who seem secure."

▪ Study what Jesus said about eternity. For example, the
Sermon on the Mount is filled with eternal perspective.

▪ Read the book of Revelation to see what is going to
happen at the end of the story.

▪ Walk through graveyards and take a look at the tomb-
stones, notice how short the time is between the dash.

▪ Read history, noting that some of the most important and
successful people in history have been completely forgotten today, and contrast that with what God promises to
those who invest in eternal things.

Developing an eternal perspective will shape your daily decisions
and priorities. Knowing that we have billions of years of existence ahead of us will inspire you to develop habits that lead to
eternal rewards.

Share the Gospel

In 150 years from now, every single person on this planet will
be in one of two places for eternity: heaven or hell. I find that
fact both incredibly exciting and deeply sobering. An eternal
perspective drives me to take the gospel to as many people as
I possibly can. It also inspired the Apostle Paul, who said in
II Corinthians 5:11, "Since, then, we know what it is to fear the
Lord, we try to persuade others."

There is no question that the Apostle Paul and the apostles
possessed an eternal perspective, and therefore were passionate
about proclaiming Christ and persuading as many people as
they could. Paul went on to say in II Corinthians 5:15-16, "And
he died for all, that those who live should no longer live for
themselves but for him who died for them and was raised again.
So from now on we regard no one from a worldly point of view."

Because Paul viewed everyone from an eternal point of view, he said in I Corinthians 9:16, "For when I preach the gospel, I cannot boast, since I am compelled to preach. Woe to me if I do not preach the gospel!"

So, in light of eternity, step out in faith and begin to talk to your friends and neighbours about Jesus. You may want to read books like *God Space* by Doug Pollock, or *I Once Was Lost*, by Don Everts and Doug Schaupp, *Questioning Evangelism* by Randy Newman, or *Turning Everyday Conversations into Gospel Conversations* by Bennett Leslee, Jimmy Scroggins, and Steve Wright to learn tips on how to share your faith.

There are also some great apps, like The Jesus Film Project App, which has the Jesus film and a number of other evangelistic videos available in hundreds of languages. Or check out the Voke, God Tools or Yes He Is apps, three fantastic resources to equip you to share your faith.

You may want to start a seeker study such as the Alpha course or Christianity Explored.

Another great opportunity is to get involved in online evangelism. The Life Project (https://thelifeproject.com/), for example, is a digital evangelism ministry that connects with millions of people every year through their online mentoring platform. Through this ministry, you can engage in gospel conversations with people from all over the world. This is a great way to gain experience in sharing your faith, which will give you more confidence to share with the people you meet in person every day. Go to https://tmm.io/ to get started!

Focus on the Great Commission

An eternal perspective will allow us to not only think about sharing Jesus with our friends and family, but will also drive us to take the gospel to those who have never heard. Jesus commanded us in the Great Commission of Matthew 28:18-20 to make disciples of all nations. He wants people all over the world to know him, and yet today, 2000 years after Jesus gave us that command, there are still 3.1 billion people who have not even heard the gospel. In light of eternity, this is tragic! We will discuss more about this later in the book.

Invest your Money in Things that will Last

Another area that will be significantly impacted by an eternal perspective is how we spend and invest our money. Randy Alcorn tells a great story about Confederate money to illustrate how to think about money in light of eternity. In the 1800s, the United States experienced a Civil War between the North (the Union Army) and the South (the Confederate Army).

> Imagine for a moment that you are alive at the very end of the Civil War. You are living in the South, but your home is really in the North. While in the South you have accumulated a good amount of Confederate currency. Suppose you also know for a fact that the North is going to win the war, and that the end could come at any time. What will you do with your Confederate money?
>
> If you were smart, there is only one answer to the question. You would cash in your Confederate currency for U.S. currency—the only money that will have value once the war is over. You would keep only enough Confederate currency to meet your basic needs for that short period until the war was over and the money would be worthless.[5]

It is easy for us to forget that all of our wealth on this planet is "Confederate currency" and will be completely worthless to us in 150 years. Yet we can exchange it for "eternal currency" that will last forever. How we invest our wealth and resources in this life will affect our return on investment in heaven. And Jesus promised an amazing return on our eternal investments.

5   Eternal Perspective Ministries. 2010. "Investing in Eternity." *Resource*. Accessed December 1, 2018.
     https://www.epm.org/resources/2010/Mar/29/investing-eternity/,

Luke 6:38,

> Give, and it will be given to you. A good measure, pressed down, shaken together and running over, will be poured into your lap. For with the measure you use, it will be measured to you.

There is a question that I am often asked that seems silly to me in light of eternity: Should I tithe off of my gross (before tax) or net (after tax) income? Jesus says that the measure you use is what will be given back to you. So going back to that Google analogy, if you knew that your investment was going to increase over 48,000 times, how much money would you want to invest? Just 10%? Or everything you possibly could?

Paul reminds us in II Corinthians 9:6-7, "Remember this: Whoever sows sparingly will also reap sparingly, and whoever sows generously will also reap generously. Each of you should give what you have decided in your heart to give, not reluctantly or under compulsion, for God loves a cheerful giver."

Where should we give? I think there are several great options, but let me highlight a few.

Give to your local church

This is God's primary vehicle for his Body on earth, and you are being ministered to there, so it makes sense that you invest there.

Give to the poor

"Truly I tell you, anyone who gives you a cup of water in my name because you belong to the Messiah will certainly not lose their reward" (Mark 9:41). And in Luke 14:13-14, Jesus says, "But when you give a banquet, invite the poor, the crippled, the lame, the blind, and you will be blessed. Although they cannot repay you, you will be repaid at the resurrection of the righteous."

Consider sponsoring a child through Compassion, or giving to other Christ-centered charities that focus on helping the poor around the world, such as Global Aid Network (GAiN). Also, in light of eternity, let me encourage you to invest in charities that not only meet the physical needs of the poor, but also focus on their spiritual needs, including giving them a chance to hear a clear presentation of the gospel.

Give towards fulfilling the Great Commission

While you may not be able to go to countries where people have never heard the gospel, there are many ways to invest in the Great Commission.

- Invest in a friend who is going on a missions project or long-term assignment.
- Invest in national workers who are ministering in their countries. Many Christian workers in the developing world struggle with having enough financial support, and in many cases, need only a few hundred dollars a month to meet all of their needs. Contact ministries like Cru (Power to Change in Canada) or the Navigators or Pioneers or SIM or other internationally-focused ministries and ask how you can support a staff member in another nation.

Invest Your Time in Eternal Things

Finally, in light of eternity, consider investing your time in things that will last eternally. This could mean volunteering at your church, or serving the poor. It might mean taking a week to go on a missions trip somewhere in the world (in light of eternity, prioritize trips where you have the opportunity to share the gospel). You may want to choose to move into a home that is located in a neighborhood that is less reached or poor so that you can have a ministry in that area. Move In (www.movein.to) is a great ministry that encourages people to do just that.

For some of you, this might mean taking a few months or

even a year away from your job and investing your full-time efforts in sharing the gospel and making disciples. Or maybe you seek opportunities to get a job in a country that is less-reached with the gospel. Perhaps your company has positions available for you to move overseas for a few years. Or it might mean that your early retirement is to free you up to engage more deeply in Kingdom-advancing ministry.

It might even mean that you sacrifice your career plans to focus full-time on helping to advance the fulfillment of the Great Commission. Sometimes, students think that since they studied medicine or engineering for four years, they automatically should spend the next 40 years in that career. That might be true, if God is calling you clearly to pursue that career, or to use those skills to give you access to restricted-access countries. But, be open to the idea that God might ask you to give that up. In light of eternity, those four or five years may not carry as much weight in your career choice. As one man said, "if God is calling you to be a missionary, do not stoop to become a king."[6]

Jesus said in Matthew 19:29,

> And everyone who has left houses or brothers or sisters or father or mother or children or fields [or careers] for my sake will receive a hundred times as much and will inherit eternal life.

Whatever lifestyle and career God calls you to, remember Colossians 3:23-24:

> Whatever you do, work at it with all your heart, as working for the Lord, not for human masters, since you know that you will receive an inheritance from the Lord as a reward. It is the Lord Christ you are serving.

In Randy Alcorn's book, *In Light of Eternity*, he quotes a section

---

6   Grow Church. 2018. "71 Famous Missionary Quotes: The Great Commission Call". Accessed Nov 30, 2018 https://growchurch.net/famous-missionary-quotes-the-great-commission

from Richard Baxter's book, *The Saints' Everlasting Rest.* I found
it deeply challenging:

> If there be so certain and glorious a rest for the saints, why is
> there no more industrious seeking after it? One would think,
> if a man did but once hear of such unspeakable glory to be
> obtained, and believed what he heard to be true, he should
> be transported with the vehemency of his desire after it, and
> should almost forget to eat and drink, and should care for
> nothing else, but how to get this treasure. And yet, people
> who hear of it daily, and profess to believe it as a fundamental
> article of their faith, do as little mind it, or labor for it, as if
> they had never heard of any such thing, or did not believe
> one word they hear.[7]

Most of us will live less than 100 years on this sin-stained,
pain-filled, guilt-ridden, violent and hateful planet. Material
possessions, career successes, and positions of prestige and power
that we gained in this lifetime will most likely be meaningless
150 years from now. But the investments of our time, talent
and treasure that we make in the Kingdom and eternal things
will provide a return on investment that is spectacular and
everlasting. Through these investments, we will bring great glory
to God, and ensure that we will receive amazing rewards that
will last for millions of years.

So, in light of that, I am begging you. Please. Think eternally
and live accordingly.

---

7   Alcorn, Randy. 1999. *In Light of Eternity.* Colorado Springs: Waterbrook Press. pg 145

CHAPTER 5

Change the Trees

Matthaios and Shimon grew up in the same Middle Eastern region, but they were not friends. In fact, they hated each other. These two men were on opposite sides politically, but they had two things in common: they were both passionate about their chosen paths, and were both willing to do whatever it took to accomplish their aims.

Matthaios worked in the area of taxation for the occupying nation that was oppressing his own people. To get to where he was in his career, he had to be hard working, driven, and willing to be hated by just about everyone. He was comfortable bullying, harassing, and sometimes even physically assaulting people to collect as much tax revenue as possible. He and his employer had a unique "profit-sharing" plan: Matthaios was given a revenue target that he was expected to collect for the government. He was then allowed to charge whatever "fees" he wanted, guaranteeing a hefty profit for himself. And he was free to collect the money by just about any means possible; the government would look the other way. People in his line of work made a lot of money . . . and a lot of enemies.

While Matthaios chose to collaborate with the government, Shimon wanted to overthrow it. Shimon was involved in a radical religious extremist group that, in its zeal, was willing to resort to violence and even assassination to accomplish its goals. Adherents of this sect were unified around a common hatred of the current government and a desire to set up their own, independent government. Of course, Matthaios and his co-workers embodied many of the reasons that Shimon and his co-conspirators hated the government, and all who were aligned with it. Self-centered, uncaring government officials showed little concern for the people they ruled, and greedy, corrupt "civil servants" used their platform to oppress citizens and line their own pockets. Shimon was certain that once the ruling government was toppled, life would be much better in his country, and he was willing to do whatever it took to ensure that this happened.

When trying to deal with people like Matthaios and Shimon, traditional methods have focused on containment (creating laws and penalties, beefing up enforcement, etc.) or elimination (imprisoning offenders, or "taking out" dangerous people through military intervention). I believe Jesus has a different solution: **Change the trees.**

Jesus made a simple, yet profound statement in Matthew 7:17-18. He said, "Every good tree bears good fruit, but a bad tree bears bad fruit. A good tree cannot bear bad fruit, and a bad tree cannot bear good fruit."

Sounds pretty straightforward, right? What do bad trees produce? Bad fruit. Why doesn't a bad tree produce good fruit? Jesus says here, "A bad tree cannot produce good fruit."

So what is Jesus' solution to this fruit problem? I believe he shares this in Matthew 12:33: "Make a tree good and its fruit will be good, or make a tree bad and its fruit will be bad." In other words, change the trees. Here's what I mean:

You probably know Matthaios and Shimon by their English names and titles: Matthew the tax collector and Simon the Zealot—two of Jesus' twelve disciples.

Jewish tax collectors in the time of Jesus were among the most hated people in society. They were collaborators with the despised Roman government, were consumed by greed, and were completely willing to bully and oppress their fellow countrymen in order to enrich themselves.

The Zealots were a Jewish extremist group that wanted to overthrow the Roman government, using violence and assassination among its methods. In other words, Simon the Zealot was a terrorist.

I find it fascinating that at least two of Jesus' 12 disciples were despicable characters who were producing some really bad fruit. But when Matthew and Simon encountered Jesus, he changed their hearts. He transformed them into "good trees," and, as a result, they were then able to produce good fruit. These angry, self-centered men became self-sacrificing disciples of Jesus, who gave their lives to introduce the world to their Lord and Savior. Jesus changed the trees.

Contrasting Fruit

In chapter two, we contrasted the fruit produced by those who are in the flesh with the fruit of those who are in the Spirit. Remember Galatians 5:19-21?

> The acts of the flesh are obvious: sexual immorality, impurity and debauchery; idolatry and witchcraft; hatred, discord, jealousy, fits of rage, selfish ambition, dissensions, factions and envy; drunkenness, orgies, and the like.

While we are often surprised at the depths of depravity of the human race, Paul explains that these actions are simply the "acts of the flesh." Or, to put it another way, bad fruit.

Immediately following this list, Paul gives us another list—a list of good fruit. In Galatians 5:22-23 NASB, he writes,

> But the fruit of the Spirit is love, joy, peace, patience, kindness, goodness, faithfulness, gentleness, self-control. Against such things there is no law.

A good tree produces good fruit, and this is the kind of fruit everybody wants to see more of!

A Better Way

I would like to suggest that the best way for us to change our
world is to focus on changing the trees. As we do that, and as
"bad trees" are transformed by the Holy Spirit into "good trees,"
our world will be changed by good fruit.

By saying this, I am not criticizing those who are trying
to bring about change through other means. I am so grateful
for the many believers who are involved in politics or trying to
bring about social justice. I have friends who serve as Members
of the Canadian Parliament, representing Jesus in the government. I have immense respect for their passionate commitment
and courage to take a stand for biblical principles for our nation.
We need Christians in our governments!

One of my heroes is William Wilberforce. Wilberforce led
an almost 50-year campaign to eliminate the slave trade in Great
Britain in the early 1800s. His long-term perseverance led to
the freeing of literally millions of slaves over the next century. I
praise God for people like him serving in leadership, and pray
that we will see more "Wilberforces" in governments all over the
world. His deep faith in God created in him a supernatural love
for the enslaved, and a deep hatred of injustice.

But I sometimes think that the Church in North America
has become overly dependent upon the government to bring
about change in our society. I have often wondered about what
our society might look like if the believers in North America had
spent less time and money lobbying for the "right" candidates
and laws, and instead focused more of our efforts on obeying
Jesus' commands to "be my witnesses" and to "make disciples of
all nations." How would our world be different if we followed
Paul's urging that "supplications, prayers, intercessions and
thanksgivings be made for all people, for kings and all who are
in high positions?"

What if, instead of vilifying the people promoting

anti-biblical values, and making them out to be our enemies, we fervently prayed for them, and practiced Jesus' command to love our enemies? What if we spent less time focusing on the "issues" and instead focused our time and energies on seeing God change the trees?

Changed Hearts Lead to Changed Values

To illustrate this, I would like to share examples of three people who were transformed by the gospel. Each of their stories are related to three prominent issues consuming our world and the Church today: abortion, human trafficking and terrorism.

Abortion

Norma McCorvey is better known by her alias, Jane Roe, the defendant in the landmark Roe vs. Wade Supreme Court case, which legalized abortion in 1973. In the late 1960s/early 1970s, a group of lawyers was hoping to legalize abortion. To accomplish this, they needed to find a test case that could eventually be brought to the Supreme Court, overturning the law that opposed abortions. Norma McCorvey would provide that test case.

Around that time, Norma was pregnant with her third child, and wanted to end her pregnancy. The lawyers persuaded her to bring a lawsuit against the US government regarding her desire to abort her own child. Though Norma was not actively involved in the case itself, Roe vs. Wade became the focal point of the abortion debate. It made it all the way to the Supreme Court, which decided to legalize abortion.

I respect the vast majority of the people who are fighting to protect unborn children, and who are currently trying to reverse the Roe vs. Wade decision. Unfortunately, there have been many pro-life advocates who have chosen to demonize anyone associated with abortion, opposing these people with bitterness and anger. But Norma experienced a different kind of response, and it changed her life.

Following the Roe vs. Wade decision in 1973, Norma began working at abortion clinics. While working at one of those clinics, she met, and became friends with, a young girl named Emily Mackey. Emily was a Christian, and her father was involved in the pro-life movement. In contrast to the hateful protesters that Norma faced, Emily and her father lived out the love of Christ in a kind and gentle fashion, and Norma became open to the gospel. Young Emily shared the gospel with Norma, who recognized her need for a savior, and gave her life to Christ.

Over the following years, as Norma grew in her faith, she began to understand how God viewed an unborn fetus—not as an impersonal tissue attached to the mother, but as a precious child of God, knitted and formed in their mother's womb. Eventually, Norma became a pro-life advocate, and gave the remainder of her life to trying to reverse the Supreme Court decision that bore her name.[1] Emily poured her efforts into changing the tree (Norma), and as Jesus changed Norma's heart, the fruit was changed.

Human Trafficking

John was involved in one of the most wicked of practices in history—human trafficking. He callously kidnapped people from their homes and smuggled them to other countries where he would sell them for his own profit, caring little of his victims' suffering. But an encounter with Jesus radically changed his life, and soon, the fruit of his life changed as well. John Newton came to understand the evils of the slave trade, and eventually became a passionate advocate for the abolition of the British slave trade in the late 1700s. He worked alongside William Wilberforce, striving to end the practice that once drove him.

1   Endroe. 2018. "The Story of Roe and Doe". *The Story of Norma McCorvey.* Accessed December 12, 2018. http://www.endroe.org/roebio.aspx

You are probably familiar with the biographical hymn that he penned, "Amazing Grace." God changed his heart, and his transformation impacted history.

Terrorism

In Jerry Trousdale's book, *Miraculous Movements: How Hundreds of Thousands of Muslims Are Falling In Love With Jesus,* a story is told of two Christian missionaries, Ahmed and Mechela, ministering in a very dangerous part of the Muslim world. One evening, they were invited by their friend Waseem to join him at a Discovery Bible Study at a nearby home. When they entered the home,

> huddled inside was a group of some thirty men. All were dressed in desert camouflage, and all were heavily armed. Several of the men had automatic rifles in their hands or within reach. Most had ammo belts draped across a shoulder, and all had unwelcoming eyes focused toward the strangers. Ahmed recognized the men as a group of rebels, whom the Western press would term, "freedom fighters."
>
> "You have heard that it was said," the rebel leader read, "'An eye for an eye and a tooth for a tooth.' But I tell you not to resist an evil person. But whoever slaps you on the right cheek, turn the other to him also." Then the leader asked, "What did Isa (Jesus) say here, in your own words?"
>
> For the next hour, the thirty men discussed the words of Jesus with Waseem, considering his commands that were so radically opposed to their own traditions, and wrestling with their conviction that they must begin to obey them. Ahmed and Mechela sat silently in a corner, gazing with amazement as many of the men, including the leader himself, wept openly over their sinful condition.
>
> "My brother," the rebel leader said in a serious tone, "our friend (pointing to Waseem) has been reading God's Word to us, and it has changed our lives." He glanced around the hut at his comrades. "We have been changed. We used to do all the stealing and . . . and other things . . . but now, we are children of God!" Many of the rebels had already given their

lives to Christ, and the group had slowly been diminishing as, one by one, the new believers returned to their homes to share the Word of God with their families.[2]

It is important to never forget about the transformative power of the gospel. In II Corinthians 5:17, the Apostle Paul explains, "If anyone is in Christ, he is a new creation. The old has passed away; behold the new has come." When Jesus truly comes into a person's life, he changes them. Paul understood this well, because this was his own story! He was transformed from being a driven, murderous religious leader into a humble, self-sacrificing servant. Jesus forgave his sins, changed his heart, and beckoned him to serve the body of Christ.

Several years ago, Guenter Lewy began to do research for a book that would defend secularism. However, the more he researched, the more he became convinced of a startling conclusion. In his book, *Why America Needs Religion,* Lewy summarized his findings: "Whether it be juvenile delinquency, adult crime, prejudice, out of wedlock births, or marital conflict and divorce, there is a significantly lower rate of such indicators of moral failure and social ills among **believing Christians.**"[3]

Simply put, I believe that when people truly follow Jesus, and allow his Holy Spirit to control their lives, the world becomes a better place.

Christianity's Impact on Society

Alvin J. Schmidt has written a fascinating and well-documented book called *How Christianity Changed the World.* In it, he describes the impact that Christianity has had on a number of significant issues in our world. For example, "the virtual lack of

---

2   Trousdale, Jerry. 2012. *Miraculous Movements: How Hundreds of Thousands of Muslims Are Falling In Love With Jesus.* Nashville: Thomas Nelson. Pg 121
3   Guenter, Lewy.1996. *Why America Needs Religion: Secular Modernity and its Discontents.* Grand Rapids: Wm. B. Eerdmans Publishing Company. pg 313

compassion for the sick and stricken among the Greco-Romans has been noted by many medical historians."[4]

Fielding Garrison, a physician and historian, says that before the birth of Christ, "The spirit toward sickness and misfortune was not one of compassion, and **the credit of ministering to human suffering on an extended scale belongs to Christianity.**"[5]

Human sacrifice was another practice impacted by Christianity:

> Sacrificing human beings for religious reasons was not confined to the pagan Canaanites and the spiritually fallen Hebrew kings. For example, the Irish, before St. Patrick had brought the Christian gospel to them, "sacrificed prisoners of war to war gods and newborns to the harvest gods." Sacrificing humans was also a common practice among the pagan Prussians and Lithuanians even until the thirteenth and fourteenth centuries. The British author Edward Ryan noted in 1802 that these people "would have done so to this day were it not for Christianity.[6]

Christian values, Schmidt goes on to explain, have played a significant role in ending the horrific practices of state-sanctioned slavery, infanticide (the killing of babies because of deformities, or of simply being undesirable) and widow burning (the practice of burning a widow alive with her deceased husband on the funeral pyre). As Christian values grow in prominence in a culture, compassion for the poor and the helpless grows, the sanctity of life is affirmed, and women are treated with greater dignity and respect.

"One scholar of ancient Rome has aptly said that 'the conversion of the Roman world to Christianity [brought] a great change in woman's status.'" Another has expressed it even

---

4   Schmidt, Alvin J. 2001. *How Christianity Changed the World.* Grand Rapids: Zondervan. Kindle Edition. (Kindle Locations 2756-2759)
5   (Ibid. Kindle location 2748)
6   (Ibid. Kindle Locations 1285-1290)

more succinctly: "The birth of Jesus was the turning point in the history of woman.'"[7]

And how do Christian values grow in a culture? By changing the trees! As people's hearts are changed by Jesus, their values will follow. A great example of this can be seen during times of revival, where God moves in a profound way among a large group of people, resulting in rapid societal transformation. Let me give you an example of this.

In the early part of the 20th century, a young Welsh college student named Evan Roberts experienced personal revival. He was so excited about what God had done in his life that he asked his pastor for a chance to speak to his church. His pastor reluctantly agreed to give him a mid-week service, to which only 17 people showed up. His sermon had only a few points: confess any known sin to God and put right any wrong done to man, put away any doubtful habit, obey the Holy Spirit promptly, and confess faith in Christ openly. That sermon was the start of something spectacular.

Dr. J. Edwin Orr, an expert in spiritual awakenings, reported that

> within three months, 100,000 converts had been added to the churches of Wales. Alcoholism dropped by 50%. Crime plummeted so much that some judges were presented with white gloves, meaning there were no crimes to try. There was even a work slowdown in the coal mines because so many workers became converted and ceased using profane language that the donkeys pulling the coal carts could not understand their instructions and had to be retrained with clean language.[8]

When God transforms the hearts of people, their values and actions follow. The new trees produce godly fruit!

---

7   (Ibid. Kindle Locations 2041-2044)
8   Hayes, Dan. 1995. *Fireseeds of Spiritual Awakening.* Orlando: Campus Crusade for Christ Integrated Resources. 25

When the Gospel is Absent

In contrast, have you ever noticed that the areas of the world that are the most volatile and dangerous are typically the parts of the world that have been the least touched by the gospel? Think about it: Right now, there are major threats in our world from Somali pirates, Middle Eastern Islamic extremists and North Korea's dictatorship. On the one hand, the gospel has not spread to these areas because it is so dangerous. But is it possible that these least evangelized areas of the world are dangerous *because* so few there have ever encountered Jesus? If an entire culture is cut off from the transforming power of the gospel and the work of the Holy Spirit, should we be surprised that the resulting culture produces bad fruit?

I find the contrast between North Korea and South Korea a striking example. In North Korea, you have an atheistic, totalitarian state. Their people are oppressed, live in abject poverty, and their dictator is constantly threatening to blow up the world. South Korea, on the other hand, was a predominantly Buddhist country in the late 1800s, but has been deeply impacted by the gospel. Millions of Koreans over the last century have risen at 4 a.m. to pray for their nation and the world. They live in a peaceful and prosperous society, and have a compassion for the world, demonstrated by the fact that they are one of the greatest missionary producing nations in history.

Darrow Miller, in his book, *Discipling Nations: The Power of Truth to Transform Cultures,* makes another intriguing observation.

> The lands in the 10/40 Window are among the poorest on earth. Many have noticed, perhaps for the first time, that the lands with the least access to the gospel are also among the neediest. This is no coincidence. While the two manifestations of secularism plus animism assert that the

problem comes from the 'outside,' biblical theism correctly holds that hunger and poverty begin inside of man.[9]

What would happen if we, as a church, began a concerted effort to pray that God works in the hearts of, for example, Islamic extremists around the world? What would happen if there was a widespread, supernatural move of God's Spirit among the people most bent on murder and destruction? What if we focused on praying for God to bring spiritual awakening to these dark, impoverished and dangerous places? What if more efforts were made to bring the gospel to these difficult and dangerous places?

I believe that God's *primary* call for the Church is to proclaim the gospel message and make disciples of all nations. That's the Great Commission! Yes, we can and should be involved in promoting biblical values in our governments and schools. But the Church's principal efforts should be focused on preaching the gospel in season and out of season (II Tim 4:2).

I don't agree with everything that Henry David Thoreau said, but he nailed it when he said, "For every thousand hacking at the leaves of evil, there is one hacking at the root."

The root problem of our world is sin. Your sin. My sin. And the sin of everyone in the world. What is the solution? The gospel of Jesus Christ! When Jesus changes a person's heart, the root is changed. Or, to put it another way, when the tree is changed, so is the fruit.

Recently, Matthew Parris, a British journalist who is also an atheist, wrote an interesting piece following a trip to Africa. He wrote,

> Now a confirmed atheist, I've become convinced of the enormous contribution that Christian evangelism makes in Africa: sharply distinct from the work of secular NGO's (non-government organizations), government projects and international aid efforts. These alone will not do. In Africa,

---

9   Miller, Darrow L. 1998. *Discipling Nations: The Power of Truth to Transform Cultures.* Seattle: YWAM Publishing. Kindle Edition. (Kindle Locations 742-746).

Christianity changes people's hearts. It brings a spiritual
transformation. The rebirth is real. The change is good.[10]

When the gospel is lived out properly, even atheists acknowledge
the impact!

The power of the gospel to change the world flows from the
transformational work of the Holy Spirit in the hearts and lives
of his children. He changes the world from the inside out. Jesus
said, "Make a tree good, and its fruit will be good."

Do you want to change the world? Focus on changing the
trees.

---

10 Greer, Peter and Horst, Chris 2014. *Mission Drift: The Unspoken Crisis Facing Leaders, Charities and
    Churches* in Bloomington: Bethany House Publishers. 35 quoted from "As an atheist, I truly believe
    Africa needs God". *The Times*, (UK) December 27, 2008.

CHAPTER 6

Ever-Expanding Faith

During spring break of my second year in university, I decided to take part in Operation Sonshine, a 5-day conference with Cru in Daytona Beach, Florida. During the week, nearly 1000 college and university students from across the United States got a chance to hear from some great speakers, receive some excellent training and enjoy times of worship. But the highlight of the week was our daily times of evangelism.

Multiple times throughout the week, we would hit the beach, attempting a number of evangelistic outreaches to gain people's attention. Sometimes we played slow-motion football, a hilarious football skit that would always gather large crowds. Other times we worked with Christian cover bands, who would perform classic rock tunes at beach hotel parties. They would play their set, which included songs about relationships or the emptiness of life, and then at one point during the show, transition over to us to begin spiritual conversations with those around us. Another time we hosted a 3 on 3 basketball tourney on the hard sand of the beach (I have a scar under my chin in a losing effort at that one). But most of the time, we would simply strike up a spiritual conversation with students who were hanging out at the beach or by a pool. It was a fun, stretching and stimulating week, and we saw God grow our faith in huge ways during that time.

On the first day of the conference, one of my friends from Baylor (I'll call him Peter), told me that during the week, he wanted to get out of his comfort zone so he could trust God in a bigger way. I was a bit more experienced in evangelism than him, so when he asked me to help him do this, I readily agreed.

As the week wore on, I kind of forgot about that challenge, but Peter didn't.

On the last day of the conference, we had wrapped up our evangelism time, and now we were just relaxing on the beach, casually chatting and celebrating after an intense week. Just then, a huge bus pulls up, accompanied by a few large and scary looking bikers on Harley Davidson motorcycles. Apparently, these guys were in Daytona Beach for Biker Week, and they had decided to spend some time on the beach—right next to where we were hanging out. They fit all of the stereotypes of bikers; they were intimidating!

Then my friend nudges me and says, "There's the challenge."

On the outside, I played it cool. After all, I was the more seasoned evangelist who was going to "help" my friend get over his fear. "Sure," I said, not sure what I was walking in to. "Let's go talk to them."

But on the inside, I was freaking out! "Are you kidding me?!" I thought. "These guys are huge, scary, and probably not terribly open to talking about Jesus. On top of that, we could be killed!"

However, I had promised Peter that I'd help him step out of his comfort zone (and now, mine!). So we grabbed a couple of gospel booklets, and walked over to talk with them. Did I mention that these guys were huge and scary? My memory may not be perfect, but from what I remember, it seemed like each of these guys were about 6' 6" and 350 pounds.

I introduced myself to the first behemoth, I mean, biker. "Hi, my name is Gregg, and this is my friend Peter."

"My name is Mountain," he replied.

"Nice to meet you, Mountain," I said, trying to hide the fact that I was shaking all over.

I reached out to shake the other guy's hand.

"My name is Animal," he said.

"Nice to meet you, Mr. Animal, Sir," I said.

I couldn't believe I was trying to have a spiritual conversation with Mountain and Animal!

I prayed as we talked with them, asking God that we would be bold, that they would be open, and that we could walk away unharmed!

We chatted for a few minutes, and then I said, "Listen guys, we are here with a group of university students, talking about how people can have a personal relationship with God. Would you be willing to take a few minutes where I could get your response to this booklet?

They agreed, and so I opened the booklet and started sharing the gospel with Mountain and Animal. Over the next few minutes, we shared how God loved them and wanted to have a relationship with them. How did they respond? Well, I'd like to tell you that they broke down in tears and repentance, but the real story is that they were just not that interested in what we had to say. But that didn't matter. God had another priority for this encounter—to grow our faith! Peter and I had stepped out of our comfort zone and shared the gospel with Mountain and Animal! And let me tell you, after sharing the gospel with these two scary giants, *we weren't afraid of anybody!*

I believe that God uses people of faith to accomplish his purposes. But how do we grow our faith?

What Is Faith?

First of all, what is faith? Many people equate faith with belief, while others describe faith as a blind leap. But the best definition I have heard for faith is "belief put into action." Let me give you an example from everyday life.

Several months ago, I took a flight from Toronto, Ontario, to Phoenix, Arizona with Air Canada. When I booked that flight, I was exercising faith in a number of things. First, I trusted that when I arrived at the airport, the flight I booked would take me to Phoenix and not, say, Baghdad. When I paid with my credit card, I trusted that Air Canada was going to charge me exactly what they said they would, and that they wouldn't use my card to buy things without my permission. I trusted that the plane was going to leave on the day and time that it said it was (or at least pretty close), and that my bags, which I handed to a stranger with Air Canada in Toronto, would arrive with me when I landed in Phoenix. Finally, I took the biggest step of faith—I physically boarded the plane, and entrusted my life to the pilots, and to the engineers who designed and maintained the plane.

Every one of those actions was a step of faith. I not only believed these facts about my flight, but I acted on them. Did you notice that none of these faith steps was a total blind leap? I knew that Air Canada is a reliable airline, and that they wouldn't steal my credit card information. I knew from experience that if a flight is scheduled to fly to Phoenix, it is unlikely to end up elsewhere, and that today, plane crashes are incredibly rare. I also know that pilots must take hundreds of hours of training and retraining to ensure that they are always at their best. So my faith was well-founded.

Now let's say that I believed that all of the things above were true, but I never actually purchased a flight or boarded an airplane because I didn't trust the system or the pilots. Since my belief was never put into action, it was not faith. Faith involves an action.

Expanding Our Faith

In chapter 3, we talked about how God uses answered prayers as one way to strengthen and expand our faith. I want to take some time now to discuss three other practical ways that we can expand our faith:

1. Reading God's Word
2. Spending time with "Big God" people
3. Taking steps of faith.

1. Reading God's Word

The Word of God (the Bible) is central to our growth as believers, and to the expansion of our faith. How does the Word help us grow in our faith? First, God's Word is supernaturally powerful. Second, it helps us understand who God is (his character and qualities). And third, it tells us stories of what he has done.

The Bible is a Supernatural Book
God's Word strengthens my faith because it is supernaturally powerful. The Creator of our universe, the sovereign King of Kings, the all-knowing, all-powerful, Almighty God has put his thoughts and desires down on paper so that we, the ones created by him, can get to know him and understand his will for our lives. That's incredible!

God inspired 40 authors from a wide range of backgrounds on three different continents to write the books of the Bible over a period of 1500 years. It was written in three languages (Hebrew, Aramaic, and Greek) and covers one of the most controversial subjects known to man—the character, plans and work of God. And yet, from this wide array of authors, there is a unified picture of the God we know and love, and his overall redemptive plan for creation. It is simple enough for children to understand, yet deep enough for the most brilliant scholars in history to study it for decades. This is a powerful book that should be read, studied and memorized!

Hebrews 4:12 says,

> For the word of God is alive and active. Sharper than any
> double-edged sword, it penetrates even to dividing soul and

spirit, joints and marrow; it judges the thoughts and attitudes of the heart.

Romans 1:16 says, "For I am not ashamed of the gospel, because it is the **power** of God that brings salvation to everyone who believes: first to the Jew, then to the Gentile."

Jesus said in Matthew 4:4, "It is written: 'Man shall not live on bread alone, but on **every word that comes from the mouth of God.**'"

Jesus and his apostles frequently quoted passages from the Old Testament. They obviously valued God's Word greatly! As we study, read, memorize and apply this great book, we can become more like Jesus, see our faith grow, and be used by God for massive Kingdom impact.

The Bible Helps us Understand Who God Is

Our faith is strengthened as we understand God's character. The Bible helps us with that. It gives us insight into his nature and character. The better I understand who God is, the more I will be able to trust him. The expression "to know me is to love me" applies perfectly to God! He is truly trustworthy because of his character.

We Can Trust God Because of Who He Is

■ The God of Love

We can trust him because he is a God of love.

Psalm 136 repeatedly reminds me that "his love endures forever." I John 4:8 tells us that "God is love," and in Jeremiah 31:3 God says, "I have loved you with an everlasting love; I have drawn you with unfailing kindness."

■ A Just and Good God

We can trust him because he is a just and good God.

Psalm 140:12 says, "I know that the LORD secures justice for the poor and upholds the cause of the needy," and Psalm 9:8 says, "He rules the world in righteousness and judges the peoples with equity." Revelation 21:4 ESV promises that "he will wipe away every tear from their eyes, and death shall be no more, neither shall there be mourning, nor crying, nor pain anymore, for the former things have passed away."

■ The God of Grace

We can trust him because he is a God of grace.

Ephesians 2:8 ESV says, "For by grace you have been saved through faith. And this is not your own doing; it is the gift of God." Romans 5:20 points out that "where sin increased, grace increased all the more." And II Corinthians 8:9 says, "For you know the grace of our Lord Jesus Christ, that though he was rich, yet for your sake he became poor, so that you through his poverty might become rich."

■ The Sovereign King of Kings

We can trust him because he is the sovereign King of Kings. Job 42:2 says, "I know that you can do all things; no purpose of yours can be thwarted." Nehemiah 9:6 says, "You alone are the LORD. You made the heavens, even the highest heavens, and all their starry host, the earth and all that is on it, the seas and all that is in them. You give life to everything, and the multitudes of heaven worship you."

As we read and study God's Word, we will better understand who God is. And having an accurate view of God will strengthen our faith.

We Can Trust God Because of What He Has Done

Our faith will further be strengthened by seeing what God has done.

For example, as we read the book of Exodus, we can see how God provided for the Israelites time and time again. He changed Pharaoh's heart to allow the Israelites to leave Egypt, and even had the Egyptians give them silver and gold jewelry and clothing as they were leaving (Exodus 12:35). He parted the Red Sea to allow them to escape Pharaoh's charging army (Exodus 14) and then he provided manna to meet their daily food needs (Exodus 16). After that, he provided water from a rock—twice—so that they wouldn't die of thirst.

Our faith is strengthened when Shadrach, Meshach and Abednego are sent to a fiery furnace because they refused to bow before an idol, but then are delivered by God (Daniel 3).

We can see how God provided for the widow at Zarephath through Elijah. When she generously gave Elijah the last of her food, God miraculously provided her and her son with a bottomless supply of oil to meet all of her needs until the drought ended.

And we can see Jesus feed a multitude of 5000, walk on water and and rise from the dead. Knowing that we serve a God who consistently achieves the impossible naturally increases my faith.

2. Spending Time with "Big God" People

Another way to grow your faith is to hang around "Big God" people. Let me explain what I mean by this.

Over my lifetime, I have encountered a lot of people with a "Small God" mentality. Maybe they felt let down by God as a result of some unanswered prayers. Maybe they are skeptical that God still works supernaturally in our world today. Maybe they are fearful to let go of their security or their stuff. Or maybe their faith is still in its infancy, having never grown beyond their initial prayer for salvation.

Around 1998, I had a meeting with a high level leader with a prominent ministry in Eastern Canada. He shared his fears about the future of ministry fund-raising in his area.

"People are giving less and less to Christian causes," he said, "Churches are giving less and less to ministries like ours. And trends are showing that there will continue to be a significant drop in the number of Christians in our nation. I don't know how ministries like ours will be able to raise any money to operate in the years ahead."

I was quite surprised that this spiritual leader was so fearful, but I couldn't agree with him. So I said to him, "You've completely forgotten about the God factor!"

This person had a "Small-God" mindset. He was more influenced by his circumstances and the latest research than he was by the Word of God. And people like that can put a dampening effect on our faith.

Since that conversation, I have personally seen God provide over $100 million for Kingdom impact. When I had that conversation with that leader, we had about 20 Power to Change staff for all of Eastern Canada. Over the next few years, we saw that number swell to over 100, all of whom saw God provide all of their support. Additionally, we have seen God provide funds for thousands of students who have taken part in short-term missions all over the world. God is still able!

While there are some people with a "Small God" mentality, I prefer the company of "Big God" people. These people believe that God is still at work today. They are regularly stepping out in faith and are willing to trust God for big things. Big God people give me life and energy! Let me describe a few other qualities of these people.

Big God people's eyes are fixed on God and his Word, not their surrounding circumstances. Big God people are often optimistic, trusting him in difficult times, because they know that God is in control and that "in all things God works for the good of those who love him" (Romans 8:28).

Big God people encourage one another to trust God, and remind each other of God's love and omnipotence. Big God people regularly talk about what God is doing in and through them regarding Kingdom impact, and celebrate Kingdom work done by others.

Big God people expect to see God work in even the darkest

parts of our world, because they believe that he is ultimately the sovereign King who reigns over all the earth.

I am constantly seeking out and befriending Big God people, because they help me see God more accurately, which increases my faith, and makes me more useable for him. I am also intentional about reading the biographies of Big God people. Brother Andrew's book, *God's Smuggler*, inspired me with stories of God allowing him to smuggle Bibles into Communist countries in the 1950s and 60s. Jim Elliot's story, *Through Gates of Splendor*, ignited my passion to impact the world. It tells the story of how he and his courageous friends took the gospel to an unreached, hostile tribe in Latin America, which eventually cost him his life, but also led to this tribe being reached with the gospel, and thousands of people being inspired to enter the mission field. Bill Bright's biography, *Amazing Faith*, reminded me to keep believing God for big things. Through Dr. Bright's lifestyle of stepping out in faith, millions have had the opportunity to hear the gospel all over the world.

I have made it a habit to proactively learn from Big God people, which strengthens my faith, making me more useable for his Kingdom. But there is one habit that has grown my faith more than any other—taking steps of faith.

3. Taking Steps of Faith

I think that we can all agree that to have a consistent walk with God, there are four foundational practices: prayer, Bible study, fellowship and worship.

These are fundamental to our faith, and Christians who are walking closely with God practice these on a regular basis. But every once in awhile, you may encounter Christians who seem to have that extra "something" about them, almost like "Super Christians." They regularly see God do really cool, supernatural stuff through them, and their walk with God is a dynamic,

vibrant adventure. Do you know people like this? I know a lot of
them, and I have learned that these people have added one more
practice to their faith, which I think makes the difference.

Looking again at these four primary practices, I would draw
a line underneath them, like this:

Most Christians live their lives above the line. They are comfortable living a good Christian life, which is fine. But, as one friend
said to me, across that line is where the magic happens. We cross
that line when we take steps of faith.

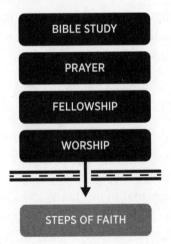

I have found that my faith has grown the most when I put
myself in a position where I need to rely fully on God. As I

proactively step out of my comfort zone, I am forced to be dependent upon God. Sometimes God puts us into situations where it is not our choice, but I have found that when I decide to prayerfully step out in faith, God shows up in cool ways. I believe this is because I am essentially saying, "God, you are worthy of my trust, so I am stepping out in faith for this situation."

Faith Barriers

One of the best things we did in our campus ministry in the early 2000's was to help students take steps of faith by sharing a concept called "faith barriers." At this point in our ministry, things were going pretty well. People were coming to faith, students were going on mission projects to different parts of the world, we were expanding to new campuses, and seeing a few new staff recruits join us. But I felt like we were missing something. Then God reminded me about faith barriers.

A faith barrier is some spiritual activity that feels like a huge roadblock to your faith. You look at it and think, "I could never do that" or "I am afraid to do that." Therefore, you need to trust God to help you get over that "barrier." Once you have broken that faith barrier, it is kind of like going to a new level on a video game—your faith is taken up a notch, enabling you to trust God for another, greater challenge. That is what my friend and I did when we approached Mountain and Animal. We stepped out in faith, and God used it to radically expand our faith.

Moses' Pattern of Breaking Faith Barriers

We can see a progression of breaking faith barriers, prompted by God, in the life of Moses. Following his 40-year exile as a shepherd, Moses has an encounter with God through a burning bush. I would say that Moses' first faith barrier was having a conversation with a bush. Of course, he learned that it was God who was speaking to him from the bush, so he wisely chose to listen.

God then tells Moses to throw his staff on the ground, and Exodus 4:3 says, "So he threw it on the ground, and it became a serpent, and Moses ran from it." I would have run too!

Immediately following this, God asks him to take the next step of faith—to pick up that snake by its tail, and it will become his staff again. For a guy who just ran from this snake, this is a much bigger step! But again, Moses obeys and picks up the snake, which turns back into his staff. His faith is expanding.

Following a few more signs, God sends Moses to talk to Pharaoh, the most powerful man in the world (and much scarier than talking with my friends Mountain and Animal). He is to ask Pharaoh to release hundreds of thousands of his slaves so they can worship God in the desert. Again, Moses obeys, and his faith grows. After that big step, God commands Moses to deliver some upsetting news—if Pharaoh doesn't let the Israelites go, God will send plagues on Egypt.

God starts delivering plagues, and keeps sending Moses to check back with Pharaoh. Can you imagine going back to Pharaoh after all of these nasty things have been happening? I imagine Pharaoh was probably not very happy with Moses. And it gets worse. Following several plagues, Moses then had to tell Pharaoh that one of those plagues will be the death of every firstborn in Egypt, including the Pharaoh's son. Again, Moses obeys and his faith is strengthened.

Finally, the Israelites are released into the wilderness. Moses thinks he's home-free, but God has yet another way to strengthen his faith—in spectacular fashion. While Pharaoh changes his mind again, and sends troops to get his slaves back, God leads Moses and the Israelites into what is essentially a corner, trapped against the Red Sea. But God commands Moses to tell the Israelites to march forward into the sea in faith, and then tells him, "And as for you, lift up your staff and stretch out your hand over the sea and divide it, and the sons of Israel shall go through the midst of the sea on dry land" (Exodus 14:16). Moses obeys again, parting the Red Sea, and the people walk through to safety.

We marvel at Moses' faith to part the Red Sea, but it all began with obeying God by throwing a stick on the ground. Each subsequent step of faith prepared him to be used by God in even more spectacular fashion.

Overcoming Faith Barriers

We began to include the faith barrier challenge in every one of our fall retreats. Near the end of the retreat, we would hand out cards that said, "By God's grace, I will trust him to _____" Students would fill out this card and place them on a board at the front of the room.

"I will pray out loud."

"I will lead a discipleship group."

"I will share my faith with my philosophy professor."

"I will go on a missions trip."

"I will go on a 1-year missions STINT in _____ (name a country)."

For people in the marketplace, their faith barriers might look like this:

"I will pray with my clients."

"I will share my faith with my business partner."

"I will give a portion of my profits to ministry."

"I will start a Bible study at my office."

"I will go on a missions trip and trust God to keep my business going while I am away."

Even more exciting was hearing the stories from these students in the months following these retreats. This revolutionized our ministry. Students (and our staff) developed a habit of trusting God for bigger and bigger things. Paralyzing fear was replaced by active steps of faith. We were developing a movement of "Big God" people.

The Big Three

Faith barriers can be any number of spiritual activities, but I have seen that there are three particular activities that put fear into almost all of us. Whenever we talk about taking faith steps in these areas, we all tend to get a bit of a sweat on our brow, a dry throat, and a slightly tightened stomach. I call them "The Big Three": Evangelism, Missions and Money:

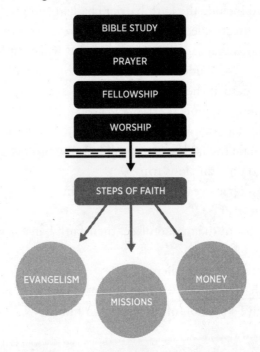

In my conversations with thousands of Christians over the years, I have found that these three areas cause the greatest fear. But I have also found that when people take steps of faith in these areas, they also produce the greatest leaps forward in our faith.

Let me tell you about how God worked in my life through one of these big three a few years ago.

When I first introduced the concept of faith barriers, I knew that as the leader, I needed to model this myself. And money was (and still is) an area in which I constantly need to trust God.

As a regional director in a large ministry, I was responsible for raising money for our various initiatives. During this time, I was seeing about $25,000/year come into our ministry, and that was from just a few donors. So I decided that I needed to take a step of faith, and attempt two big events that were going to cost an additional $20,000 ($10,000 each): a debate series and a fundraising dinner. This was a huge step of faith for me! But I made a public declaration to my staff and students that I was going to do it, and so was forced to follow through on it.

However, as the year progressed, I discovered that the two events were not going to cost $10,000 each. They would cost $15,000 each! My faith barrier had grown by 50%! My directors had approved me spending the money on both events, with the hopes that I would see the money come in during the fundraising dinner. I'd like to tell you that I was totally faith-filled and calm during this time, but I was actually a wreck. I had taken a huge financial risk, but this step of faith forced me to pray with greater intensity than I had ever done before.

As we approached the date of the fundraiser, I was talking to the guy who was coaching me in running the dinner. After explaining some of the information around how many were attending and what some of our key donors might give, I asked him "How much should I expect to raise at this dinner?"

He said $25,000.

"Great," I thought, "I just spent $30,000 on these two events,

and I am going to raise even less than that. I might lose my job!"
That led me to pray with great intensity: "God, please allow us
to raise $40,000!"

The dinner came, and the program went well. When we
added up the pledges and gifts at the end of the night, the total
amount was . . . $40,000! God came through!

At the next year's dinner, we prayed that God would provide
$60,000 . . . and we raised $60,000. The following year, we
prayed for $80,000 . . . and after our initial quick count that
evening, I was told that we had raised $77,000.

I told my assistant, "We have been praying for $80,000.
Could you go back and count again? I think we must be missing
something." She came back a few minutes later and said, "We
found another envelope that we hadn't counted the first time,
and inside was a check for $5000." We had raised over $82,000!

Today, I am asking God to allow me to raise hundreds of
millions of dollars. I am asking him to allow me to share the
gospel with CEO's and high-ranking government officials. My
faith has grown as I have matured in my faith and taken on
additional steps of faith.

Please note also that I didn't start out asking for millions
of dollars or talking with ambassadors from foreign nations. I
started by sharing my faith with some friends in my school, and
then progressed to sharing the gospel with kids in a government
housing area. I asked my church to support this ministry with
a gift of $500. I gave a gift of $50 (which I couldn't afford) to a
friend for a conference. Each of these small steps of faith prepared me for greater steps of faith later in life.

Commit to a Life of Ever-increasing Faith

I have often wondered what our world would be like if the
Church were filled with people who regularly took steps to grow

and expand their faith. I believe we would see God's Kingdom expand in ways we never imagined.

Jesus said in Matthew 17:20, "If you have faith as small as a mustard seed, you can say to this mountain, 'Move from here to there,' and it will move. Nothing will be impossible for you."

God is looking for men and women who are willing to trust him to be used supernaturally. But our faith won't grow by accident. So ask God to strengthen your faith. Seek to learn from people of strong faith from Scripture and history, and from those around you. And commit to regularly stepping out of your comfort zone, to allow God to use you beyond your natural abilities.

I am praying that God raises up thousands of "Big God" people who are consistently increasing their faith. For if we become a movement of believers with increasing faith, God will use you and me to do amazing things for his glory.

CHAPTER 7

The Power of Multiplication

I was in my last year of university, and I was really confused. I was about to graduate, but I had no idea about where I was going to invest the next several years of my life. I felt pretty confident that God was calling me to ministry, but I didn't know where or to what type of ministry. I saw needs everywhere, and each potential option possessed its own compelling reasons to pursue it. God had given me a heart for many different areas, so I wasn't sure where to begin.

My first option was doing **inner city** ministry. During my first few years at Baylor, I had poured myself into ministering in the government housing projects close to our campus. This was complex and challenging work, and gave me a deep appreciation of the immense needs among the marginalized. Perhaps, God was calling me to this type of work.

Out of this work grew a love for **African Americans**. God had given me a special love for the black kids I worked with in the projects, and I had always loved the African American culture. Maybe it was because I felt my black friends were simply cooler than me. I was intrigued by the opportunity to continue ministering among this community, but how could I do that?

Another area that was compelling me was the **Muslim** world. Not only were Muslims difficult to reach, there weren't very many people even trying to reach them. At that time, it was explained to me that the number of missionaries focusing on reaching Muslims was about one for every million Muslims. I wanted to help! "Perhaps," I thought, "I should go work in the Muslim world."

Eastern Europe created another tug. This was during the

late 1980s, when communism was beginning to fall. The Eastern European people, having been starved of any spiritual input for decades, had an immense hunger for spiritual truth. I knew there was a unique window of opportunity here that wouldn't last forever, so this was not an opportunity to be missed.

Beyond these options, I recognized the needs among **youth and university students**. I had learned that 85% of the people who made decisions to receive Christ did so before the age of 18, so youth work made a lot of sense. I also understood the strategic nature of university students—they are more open to new ideas than at any time in their lives, they are often the leaders of tomorrow, and they are in the process of making major life decisions. Should I maybe pursue working among these groups?

On top of all of these options, I understood that the **local church** was God's primary means for impacting the world, so I wanted to seriously consider that as well. I wasn't ready for seminary yet, but perhaps I could find ways to serve in a local church.

Too Many Options!

I wanted to have an impact on ALL of these areas—inner city, African Americans, the Muslim world, Eastern Europe, youth, university students and church. Can you identify with this? Each of these areas represented significant needs, and each of them drew me at some level. But there was no way I could reach them all. . . or was there?

You may remember how, at the beginning of this book, I shared about being blown away at the colossal needs of the small, island nation of Haiti. As an idealistic 18 year old, I had wanted to change the world, but after visiting a slum area of 200,000 people, and seeing the immense needs, my dream seemed impossible. And those 200,000 people only represented a very small part of the 8 million people who lived in Haiti, not

to mention the 5 billion people who lived on the planet at that
time.

Today, we live on a planet with 7.5 billion people. India's
population alone grows by approximately 1.2 million people
every month![1] So how in the world can we even dream of having
a global impact?

Jesus' Master Plan

When Jesus gave his Great Commission in Matthew 28:18-20,
he included a strategy that would allow these disciples to have a
massive, global impact: spiritual multiplication. Note that Jesus
did not just command them to "make disciples." Let's look at
the verse again.

> Therefore go and make disciples of all nations, baptizing
> them in the name of the Father and of the Son and of the
> Holy Spirit, and **teaching them to obey everything I have
> commanded you.** And surely I am with you always, to the
> very end of the age.

When Jesus said, "teaching them to obey everything I have
commanded you," that included his command to make disciples
of all nations. In other words, don't just make disciples. Jesus
told his disciples to make disciples who make disciples who
make disciples who . . . You get the picture.

Paul explained this spiritual multiplication concept even
more clearly in II Timothy 2:2:

> "And the things you (Timothy) have heard me (Paul) say in
> the presence of many witnesses entrust to reliable people (RP)
> who will also be qualified to teach others (O)."

---

1   Worldometers. 2018. World Population. Accessed November 30, 2018 http://www.worldometers.
info/world-population/india-population/.

2 Timothy 2:2

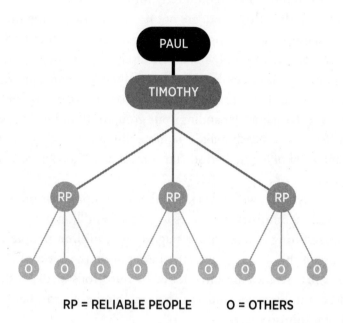

RP = RELIABLE PEOPLE   O = OTHERS

The concept of spiritual multiplication represents one of the most powerful, far-reaching strategies that Jesus gave his Church. In fact, the long-term, multiplied impact that a single, multiplying disciple can have over a lifetime is staggering. Once I understood this, it changed everything.

A Hypothetical Competition

To explain the incredible reach of this approach, I want to set up a hypothetical "competition" between you and me regarding the number of people impacted by two different methods.

In this scenario, let's say that I am a really amazing ministry superstar who speaks to thousands of people at a time (a stretch, I know). In fact, each year through my preaching ministry, I am able to impact over 1 million people for Christ. So after two years, I have impacted 2 million people. After 5 years, I've reached 5 million, and so on. Pretty impressive, eh?

You, on the other hand, are not nearly as gifted as me (in this scenario!). Not having the same oratorical skills that I possess, you decide to simply make one disciple, with the objective of equipping that disciple to make one disciple themselves. After your first year, there are two of you. The second year, each of you make a disciple, expanding your group to four. During year 3, the four of you each make one more disciple, bringing you to a grand total of eight. And so you continue . . . slowly: 16, 32, 64, 128, etc.

After 15 years, we get back together to compare our progress. My speaking ministry continues to impact a million people a year, resulting in a reach of a staggering **15 million people**! Because of this amazing ministry, I am put on the cover of *Christianity Today*. I am interviewed by numerous media outlets. And I am in huge demand as a speaker. In other words, I am a rock star ministry guy!

You, on the other hand, continue plodding along, making disciples who make disciples. The results? Not nearly as impressive at this point. While I have reached 15 million people, your multiplied impact has grown to reach a little more than 32,000 people. Respectable, yes, but not headline grabbing. In fact, because most of the work has been happening *through* these other multiplying disciples, almost no one even knows that you had any part in this.

We continue with our respective approaches, and after year 33, we meet up again. I have continued to have an impact on 1 million people a year, allowing me to touch 33 million people, which is equivalent to a medium sized country!

How about you? Well, as you and your multiplying disciples continued making one multiplying disciple per year, after 33 years your "discipleship chain" has grown to over 8 billion! Wow!! The Great Commission is completed! Hallelujah!

Now, obviously, this is a hypothetical scenario, where everything worked perfectly. But there is no denying the power of multiplication. Check out these numbers below:

YEAR	SPIRITUAL ADDITION	SPIRITUAL MULTIPLICATION	
1	1,000,000	2	
2	2,000,000	4	
3	3,000,000	8	
4	4,000,000	16	
5	5,000,000	32	
6	6,000,000	64	PEOPLE REACHED
7	7,000,000	128	
8	8,000,000	256	
9	9,000,000	512	
10	10,000,000	1,024	
15	15,000,000	32,768	
20	20,000,000	1,048,576	
25	25,000,000	33,554,432	
33	33,000,000	8,589,934,592	

In the illustration above, you can see the difference between spiritual addition and spiritual multiplication over the long term. In the illustration below, you can see it represented graphically.

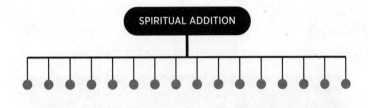

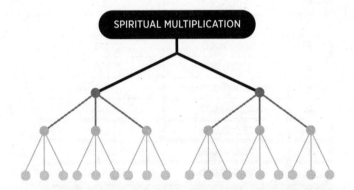

Jesus commanded his disciples to make multiplying disciples.
I believe that one of the reasons for this was because spiritual
multiplication is the fastest and most effective way to reach the
greatest number of people in the shortest period of time. In fact,
I believe that if the Church had followed this one directive over
the centuries, we would have finished the Great Commission
several times over by now.

Hindrances to Spiritual Multiplication

So why don't more Christians practice this? I think there are
several reasons, but let me touch on three.

First, many people lack the confidence to do this. They think that they are not smart enough or spiritually mature enough to make disciples. But note the simple requirement that Paul gives Timothy in II Timothy 2:2, "And **the things you have heard me say** in the presence of many witnesses entrust to reliable people who will also be qualified to teach others."

What was Timothy asked to entrust to his disciples? The things he had learned from Paul. He was expected to take what he learned and pass it on to others.

I believe that the second reason Christians give up on this is that spiritual multiplication initially moves *really* slowly. Look at the numbers those first few years: 2, 4, 8, 16. For really gifted teachers or charismatic leaders, these numbers seem boring! Why build into just one or two, when you can build into hundreds? It may make sense that because the needs are so great we may feel a compassion-driven urgency to reach out to as many as we can, as quickly as we can. But it is important that we keep focused on the long-term results of this approach.

A third reason that Christians don't practice this is simply because they have fallen away from the faith. We are in a spiritual battle, and Satan will use whatever he can to destroy Christians' faith or to lessen their effectiveness. And I believe, keeping Christians from multiplying is one of Satan's top priorities.

Ironically, I have personally found that one of the things that has kept my faith strong is my ongoing focus on discipling others. There is built-in accountability when I am building into others. I need to pray for them, answer their questions, and help them grow. This, in turn, forces me to spend time in God's word to make sure I know what I am talking about. We pray together. We do ministry together. And we encourage one another in our faith. All of these things generally keep me focused on my own walk with Jesus.

Spiritual Multiplication - A Case Study

We can see that spiritual multiplication works extremely well in theory, but how about in real life? From my experience, I'd say pretty well. Here's my story.

At the beginning of this chapter, I spoke about my confusion as I tried to discern which of several areas I should focus my ministry efforts on: the inner city, African Americans, Muslims, Eastern Europe, youth, university students and churches. Well, during my fifth year in full-time ministry, it dawned on me that through making disciples at the University of Georgia (UGA), God had allowed me to touch every one of these areas. Let me explain how.

In my third year at UGA, I began discipling Jasper. Jasper was one of the most influential **African American** students on campus, in part because his father was a prominent and well-known pastor in Atlanta. Jasper used his influence to open doors with other African American students, and the ministry began to gain momentum. Jasper began discipling David, an outgoing and teachable young leader with whom I enjoyed a deep and almost immediate connection. Jasper went on to co-pastor (with his father and brother) a predominantly African American church in Atlanta with over 11,000 people. Today, Jasper is lead pastor at a predominantly African American **church** that he and his wife planted, also in Atlanta, and speaks to many audiences across the US and around the world. David went on to become a pastor of a predominantly black church in inner-city Cleveland. Recently, he was invited to be a part of the governor's commission on race relations for the state of Ohio. God was allowing me to to impact African Americans through the young men I had discipled.

Another African American student I discipled was Dorian. I had introduced Dorian to faith through a conversation about "changing the trees." As Dorian grew in his faith, he led friends to faith, and took part in a summer missions project with our ministry to **inner city** Los Angeles. The following year, Dorian recruited a few other African American students to take part in that project as well. Of course, as African Americans, their influence on black youth would be much more profound than anything I could ever do. Through Dorian and some of his friends, I was impacting the inner city.

Erik was in his first year when he was introduced to faith by Mike, a student I was discipling. As I discipled Erik, he grew quickly and was passionate about sharing his faith. He loved stepping out of his comfort zone, and began to gain a vision for the world. So I challenged him to go on a summer missions trip to a Muslim nation, which was one of the least reached nations in the world. He enjoyed that project so much that he committed to returning the following year for a one-year STINT. Erik spent that next year recruiting several students to join him, and during their STINT, their team was able to introduce many **Muslims** to faith. In an amazing providential addition to this story, I recently met one of the people whom Erik had led to faith that year. Baskin (for his safety, I have changed his name) was led to faith and discipled by Erik during his year in that country. Today, Baskin continues to introduce Muslims to Jesus and has helped plant five churches in that nation!

Jay, another guy I discipled from the University of Georgia, went on to give leadership to a summer missions project in **Eastern Europe**, helping students share the gospel during this spiritually ripe time in history. Roy went on a missions project to Western Europe.

Drew went on to become a **youth** pastor. In fact, over the next several years, Drew trained dozens of other youth pastors. I asked him once what he was training his guys in. His response? "I'm just teaching them the things you taught me—the Spirit-filled life, initiative evangelism, the Great Commission, spiritual multiplication, etc."

Jay, Erik and Eric (another UGA guy I discipled) joined staff with our ministry and worked for several years with **university** students, sharing the gospel and discipling men on campus.

I was only at the University of Georgia for four years, but through spiritual multiplication, God allowed me to touch every one of the areas that he had laid on my heart. Spiritual multiplication works!

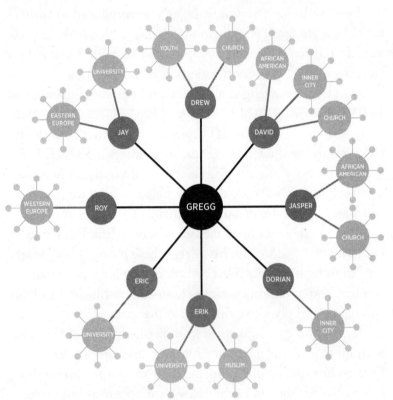

Be Fruitful and Multiply

When God created Adam and Eve, his first command to them as a couple was "Be fruitful and multiply." When Noah and his family exited the ark after the flood, God's first command to them was "Be fruitful and multiply." And when Jesus gave his final command to his disciples before his ascension, he commanded them to make disciples who make disciples. In other words—be fruitful and multiply!

Let's Get Practical

So how do we do this?

I'd like to suggest five simple steps:

1) Ask God to allow you to multiply
2) Be intentional about being discipled and discipling others
3) Ensure your training is transferable
4) Allow others to help you multiply
5) Be thinking always of ways to multiply

Ask God To Allow You to Multiply

As we explored in chapter 3, I John 5:14-15 says,

> This is the confidence we have in approaching God: that if we ask anything according to his will, he hears us. And if we know that he hears us—whatever we ask—we know that we have what we asked of him.

We can be confident that becoming a spiritual multiplier is completely within God's will, because Jesus commanded everyone to do this in his Great Commission. Spiritual multiplication is a *spiritual* activity, so ultimately, God is the one who will allow us to multiply. So ask God to allow you to multiply!

Be Intentional About Being Discipled and Discipling Others

Seek out an older, more mature believer who can help you grow in your walk with God. This is not always easy, but if you are in

college or university, I have found that one of the best ways to
do this is to become a part of a larger ministry. Ministries like
Cru (Power to Change in Canada), InterVarsity and Navigators,
for example, can provide mature leaders, helpful frameworks,
and proven tools to aid you in your multiplication. Many
churches have discipleship programs that you can plug into.
This will prepare you to disciple others.

If you are a more mature believer, seek out people to disciple.
How do you find people to disciple? The key is evangelism. I
remember talking with a young woman who lived in a large
apartment building. She was lamenting that although she
wanted to lead a Bible study in her building, there weren't any
Christians living there. Wanting her to see that there was an
alternative, I said, "You could . . . make some." In other words,
the best way to find disciples is to share the gospel with lots of
people. As you do that, there are three positive outcomes that
could help you make disciples:

1) You will meet seekers who are looking for someone to help
them explore faith issues.
2) You will surface Christians who want to grow in their faith.
3) You will introduce people to our Savior.

In each of these scenarios, you will be helping people along in
their spiritual journey, eventually making disciples who can
make disciples.

Ensure Your Training is Transferable

One key element in multiplying yourself is ensuring that your
training is easily transferable from one person to the next.

When I was in university, I would take the guys I was discipling out to share the gospel. I had some experience in sharing
my faith, so I would talk with other students about Jesus in a
free-flowing conversation, hoping to help them understand the

gospel. After these conversations, I would debrief with the guys I was "training," which usually went something like this:

Me: "So, how do you think that went?"
Disciple: "That was cool! You were pretty good at that!"
Me: (trying to act humble), "Thank you. So, do you think you could do that?"
Disciple: "Never! You are just naturally good at that, so I won't even try."

I found myself pretty disappointed by all of this, as I really wanted to multiply myself. When I first joined staff with Cru in the late 1980s, I was asked to use a transferable gospel booklet (today called *Knowing God Personally*) during my times of evangelism. This well-known evangelism tool was widely used by our staff and students, but I resisted using tools such as this, as they felt "canned." However, wanting to be a compliant new staff member, I agreed to start using the booklet. During my first nine weeks on campus, **I introduced a student to faith each week!**

Aside from the fact that I was able to introduce a number of students to faith through this tool, I found that I was actually able to easily train others in how they could share Christ with others. For example, I trained Mike, a first year student, in how to share his faith using this tool, and he led his friend Erik to faith. After Erik began to grow in his faith, I took him out to share the gospel, and he watched me share a gospel booklet with another student. During our debrief, our conversation went like this:

Me: "So, how do you think that went?"
Erik: "That was cool! That guy was pretty open."
Me: "Do you think you could do that?"
Erik: "All you did was read the book. I can do that!"

Over the next few months, Erik used that tool to lead his

mother, his sister, and a few friends of his to faith. I had
successfully multiplied myself!

I share that story not to promote any particular tool, but to
demonstrate the value of using a transferable tool to multiply
yourself. Tools such as these can provide a clear and repeatable
framework that can help you equip others to have an effective
ministry. The Alpha program, for example, is a great tool used
by hundreds of thousands around the world to share the gospel.
The program is designed to make it simple for anyone to bring
friends along on a spiritual journey, and new believers can then
multiply themselves by hosting Alpha groups themselves.

You may be surprised to know that Jesus used simple, transferable tools to train his disciples. No, he wasn't carrying around
a backpack full of gospel tracts. But think about the Lord's
prayer, for example. This is a simple but profound framework
for prayer that is easily remembered, and easily passed on. I am
sure that the religious leaders of the day scoffed at this prayer
as overly simplistic. And yet, that was how Jesus trained his
disciples to pray.

How about parables? This was yet another brilliant tool that
Jesus used to communicate deep, spiritual truths to his disciples.
It is hard to remember details of a lecture about God's grace. But
it is pretty easy to remember the story of the Prodigal Son. These
stories were easy to pass on, allowing his disciples to quickly
multiply.

Of course, we need to ask God to help us genuinely love the
people we are sharing with, and not treat them as some sort of
a project. But don't shy away from utilizing tools to help you
ensure that your teaching is transferable. Just as having the right
tool can help you repair a car or fix a sink, using proven tools in
evangelism can help you to share your faith more effectively and
train others to do the same. Naturally, any tool feels awkward
when you first start using it, whether a table saw or a gospel tool,

but with time and practice, it becomes more comfortable and effortless to use it.

Today, for example, there are several apps that you can use to share your faith and train others. Some of these include God Tools (simple gospel presentations), the Jesus Film Project app (includes gospel videos in hundreds of languages), 5fish (interactive mobile app to listen to gospel messages in thousands of languages), and The Bridge app (videos to share with those with faith questions). Looking online will provide you with dozens more. As you start using these tools, you will become more proficient in sharing your faith, and then you can multiply yourself by inviting others to do the same.

Allow Others to Help You Multiply

I learned a long time ago that I am not good at everything. So, I am constantly seeking out people and resources to help me more effectively multiply. Let me give you a few examples.

Books

Allow brilliant authors to equip and inspire those you are discipling. I love to read, and have been tremendously inspired by a number of books over my lifetime. So, whenever I find a book that inspires me, I buy a few copies to give away to those I am ministering to. Here are a few books that shaped my Kingdom vision early in my career, and that I have passed on to help me multiply.

- Robert E. Coleman's book, *Master Plan of Evangelism,* helped me to understand Jesus' framework and vision for discipleship and spiritual multiplication.
- Elisabeth Elliot's *Through Gates of Splendor* and Brother Andrew's *God's Smuggler* both expanded my vision for missions. John Piper's *Let the Nations Be Glad* provided

me with the theological foundation for missions, and his
book *Finish the Mission* inspired me with an urgency to
continue to press on to help fulfill the Great Commission.

▪ Dan Hayes' *Fireseeds of Spiritual Awakening* inspired me
with stories of young people being used to impact the
world for Jesus. I have given away hundreds of copies of
this book in an effort to inspire others.

Guest speakers

I would occasionally invite a missionary or an inspiring leader to
join my discipleship group to share stories, cast vision or teach
our group in areas in which I am weak.

Conferences and retreats

I did everything in my power to get the guys I was discipling to
attend these events. There is something about the environment
of a group of people gathered together to learn about God and
worship him that allows God to do profound work in people's
hearts. These events provide the space for people to think more
deeply about their walk with God, and the momentum to allow
them to step out of their comfort zones to see God use them
for his glory. I knew if I could get my guys to these conferences,
their growth would be accelerated, their passion ignited, and
their ability to multiply would be enhanced.

Be Thinking Always of Ways to Multiply

There are lots of ways for us to multiply ourselves if we always
maintain a multiplier's mindset. Let me give you a few examples.

Prayer

Do you have a prayer meeting on your campus or at your
church? Simply invite a friend to join you each week, and hold

each other accountable to show up and invite others. Every time you do this, you are multiplying your impact.

Or maybe you are praying for some friends who don't know Jesus, or for a specific event coming up. Invite five to six friends to join you in praying for this.

Maybe you want to pray for your nation, or community, or some specific people group. By inviting others to join you in this, you are multiplying yourself, and acting on Jesus' advice on prayer. He said in Matthew 18:19-20, "Truly I tell you that if two of you on earth agree about anything they ask for, it will be done for them by my Father in heaven. For where two or three gather in my name, there am I with them."

Evangelism

Several years ago, I was coaching a student leader who was very effective in sharing his faith. But he often did this by himself. I would constantly encourage him to invite others along, but he preferred to fly solo, missing the opportunity to equip others and multiply himself. As a result, when he graduated, the ministry suffered, and we essentially had to start over from scratch.

Contrast him with my friend Carlos, who is in the finance industry. Carlos is one of the most fruitful evangelists I know. But not only is he regularly sharing his faith, he is also constantly training people in sharing the gospel. He has become a leader in the Alpha program, with a focus on equipping others to do what he is doing. As a result, he has launched several Alpha groups, effectively multiplying himself.

Conferences and Retreats

Are you planning on attending an upcoming conference or retreat? How many people are you planning on bringing along? Not only is it more fun to have friends join you, you are giving them the opportunity to benefit from the input as well.

Consider offering a full or partial scholarship to a friend or two to help them overcome any financial barriers to attending. Or maybe you could invite other friends or family members to help invest in your friends' spiritual growth.

Short-Term Missions

Are you going on a short-term missions project? Prayerfully invite one or two other friends to join you.

When my friend Erik decided to go to a Muslim nation for a year, he mobilized others to join him in praying for laborers for this country, and invited several to join him on the year-long STINT. By recruiting three others from his campus to go with him, he *quadrupled* his potential impact on that nation!

Another student, after returning from a missions project to East Asia, committed to pray that eight students from his campus would join him on the project the following year. He invited everyone he could, and asked others to join him in praying for this goal. The next summer, that student returned to East Asia with eight friends from his campus.

Giving

Are you giving money to a Christ-centered ministry? Invite others to match your gift. During my first year at Baylor, one of the campus ministries was encouraging students to throw their spare change into a plastic, loaf-shaped piggy bank as a way to raise money for the hungry. While many people simply threw in their nickels and dimes into this piggy bank, I decided to go to every one of the 50 guys on my residence floor, and invited each of them to give one dollar towards this cause. And everybody did! Through that multiplied effort, I was able to raise far more money than if I had just given my own money, which allowed even more hungry people get food and water.

Multiply the Doers

With the immense needs in the world, it is more important than ever that believers focus on multiplying themselves. In the late 1800s/early 1900s, the Student Volunteer Movement became one of the greatest missionary sending movements in history, mobilizing over 15,000 students into missions over 30+ years. The multiplied impact of these missionaries advanced the gospel globally like few other efforts in history.

I have been inspired by a quote from John Mott, the longtime president of the Student Volunteer Movement. He said, "He who does the work is not so profitably employed as he who multiplies the doers."[2] In other words, I can best use my time and energies by focusing on multiplication. And as we do that, the scope of our impact will be far greater than anything we imagined.

---

2   Cru.comm. 2007. "Lessons I Have Learned: John Mott." Accessed March 24, 2019. https://www.cru.org/content/dam/cru/legacy/2012/04/mottlessonsihavelearned.pdf

CHAPTER 8

Exalted in Every Nation

Do you like field trips?

I love field trips! One of my favourite field trips was when I was in the 5th grade. A small group of us were invited to go to a place called Chalk Hill in Southern California. This place had thousands of chalky rocks that you could collect. But if you split those chalk-rocks just right, inside, you could find a fossil! Unfortunately, we didn't come across any T-Rex teeth, but we did find a bunch of millenia-old leaves and bugs, which was pretty cool.

To kick off this chapter, I am going to take us on a mental field trip. I actually consider myself an expert in mental field trips, having perfected this skill during my Social Theory class in university.

An Apple Orchard

As we begin this mental field trip, we are travelling on a bus to visit a very unique apple orchard. This orchard is many, many miles in size, and has over 17,000 trees. During our drive there, the bus driver explains to us that each of these trees is massive, capable of producing thousands of apples every day. The owner of the orchard takes great care of it, ensuring that the environment is perfect for harvesting the greatest number of apples. The only problem, the bus driver tells us, is that they can never find enough people to pick or harvest the apples.

As we draw closer to the orchard, however, it seems like there are plenty of apple pickers. Every tree that you can see has hundreds of people in and around it, collecting apples. They seem to have everything they need. They've got sturdy ladders, huge buckets, and a seemingly efficient system—while some people are in the trees, there are others holding the buckets, and others driving collection vehicles. Each has their area of expertise that they can focus on.

As our bus pulls up alongside the orchard, something else stands out. There are hundreds, even thousands of people walking past the orchard. Most of these people just pass by, not bothering to even look at the trees. But on occasion, one of them sees a ripe apple and picks it, and drops it into one of the collecting buckets before they continue on their way.

Now that you are close to the orchard, you are struck by the enormous size of each of these trees. In fact, the trees are so huge that it is virtually impossible to reach the apples at the very top. But then you notice a very cool solution: there are actually helicopters hovering over the top of these trees, lowering pickers to collect the fruit that is out of reach to those on the ground. When you ask the bus driver about this, he explains that the idea and the money came from the Apple Picking Research and Development Institute. This institute is fully funded by the owner of the orchard to ensure that every ripe apple in his orchard has the opportunity to be harvested.

As you gaze at the well-orchestrated movement of thousands of apple pickers, you wonder why the bus driver says that there are not enough workers. It certainly doesn't look like there is any need for more help. Everywhere you look, there are hundreds of pickers doing great work. So you ask the bus driver why he says that there aren't enough pickers. He hands you a large bucket and the keys to a small collection vehicle, points you deeper into the orchard, and tells you to go find out for yourself.

You start making your way through the orchard. You drive for an hour, then two hours, and you continue to see pickers everywhere. But as you go deeper into the orchard, you start to notice a drop-off in the number of people. You are tempted to help them, because you can see that there is a lot of fruit to be picked. But you decide to keep going.

A few hours into your journey into the orchard, you come upon something astonishing. There, right in front of you, is an apple tree that is filled with beautiful apples, but not a single person is there to collect them. You can't believe it! So you quickly run to the tree, and begin easily grabbing the low-hanging fruit that is literally ripe for the picking.

Soon, however, you notice a problem. It is going to be impossible for you to reach the apples at the top of this tree. As you begin to think of ways of attacking this problem, you notice that near the top of the tree is a single apple that is among the most beautiful you have ever seen. You have to get that apple! But just as you are trying to figure out your next move, that apple suddenly plummets to the ground and smashes right in front of you.

"What a waste of a beautiful apple!" you exclaim. But now something else catches your attention. As you look around on the ground, you see mounds of over-ripe apples that have fallen and decayed. With no one to pick the fruit, these once-perfect apples had become over-ripened and crashed to the ground, wasted.

Next, just as you are contemplating this sad scenario, you look around you, and what you see completely overwhelms you. Everywhere you look, as far as you can see, there are actually thousands of apple trees—and not one of them has a single picker. There, in the midst of your quiet solitude, you hear over and over, the repeated, sickening thud of over-ripened apples falling to the ground, wasted.

As you further study the situation, you begin to understand why some trees have no one there. Several are difficult to get to, like the ones located on an island in the middle of a raging river, or the ones right on the edge of a steep cliff. Others are filled with angry and aggressive hornets' nests. And still others are guarded by huge, snarling packs of wild dogs. But many of these trees have no barriers, and have low-hanging fruit that could be picked very easily.

What can you do? The task is far too great for you to handle, so you begin to work your way back towards the bus with your single, full bucket. You are filled with emotions that range from confusion to sadness to anger. "Why are all the workers bunched together?" you wonder.

On your drive back to the bus, you encounter multiple pickers arguing about who "owns" a single tree, elbowing each other out of the way to collect more apples. After seeing this happen around several different trees, you want to scream, "Why don't you go to the areas where there are no pickers?!?!" Instead, you keep going, and pick up your pace, hurrying back to the bus.

You find yourself wondering what the owner thinks about this. All of the money and people focused on the easily accessible part of the orchard are obviously worth it, as many apples are being successfully harvested. But you keep thinking of all of those unharvested trees surrounded by now-dead apples.

As you arrive back at the bus, you hand your bucket to the driver, and tell him that although you don't have much training, you want to help. He smiles broadly and asks you a simple question: "Where do you want to start picking?"

Is the Great Commission Found Only in One Passage?

By now, you may have figured out that this story is an allegory for the current state of the Great Commission.

The Great Commission is something that has been heard about by most Christians, understood by many, embraced by some, and acted on by very few.

Jesus gave the Great Commission to his disciples in Matthew 28:18-20:

Then Jesus came to them and said, "All authority in heaven
and on earth has been given to me. Therefore go and make
disciples of all nations, baptizing them in the name of the
Father and of the Son and of the Holy Spirit, and teaching
them to obey everything I have commanded you. And surely I
am with you always, to the very end of the age."

When I was younger, I often wondered why everyone made such
a big deal out of this one passage of Scripture. There are lots
of commands in Scripture, why was this one singled out as so
important?

What I did not realize at the time was that this was not the
first time this idea was put forth. We can trace God's global
vision all the way back to Genesis 12:3, when God told Abraham,
"I will bless those who bless you, and whoever curses you I will
curse; and **all peoples on earth will be blessed through you.**"

This theme is repeated by God many times throughout the
Old Testament, but I did not recognize it, because I did not
understand the significance of the word "nations" in the Great
Commission.

The word translated as nations is the Greek word *ethnos*.
Today, when we think about nations, we often think of borders
and formal governments, but ethnos is really talking about
people groups, which are identified by their unique language
and culture.

In the Old Testament, the Hebrew word for nations is *goyim*.
Once I understood this, it became clear to me that Matthew 28
is not the only time God talked about reaching the nations. He
actually talks about it a lot!

We see it in the oft-quoted passage, Psalm 46:10, "Be still,
and know that I am God; I will be exalted among the nations
(*goyim*), I will be exalted in the earth." This is actually a prophecy that one day God will be exalted among all *goyim*.

A similar prophecy is found in Psalm 86:9: "All the nations

(*goyim*) you have made will come and worship before you, O Lord; they will bring glory to your name."

Other related passages did not contain the word *goyim*, but communicated the same global theme:

Isaiah 49:6 says,

> It is too small a thing for you to be my servant to restore the tribes of Jacob and bring back those of Israel I have kept. I will also make you a light for the Gentiles, that my salvation may reach the **ends of the earth.**

As I looked for more Old Testament passages that included the word *goyim,* I discovered commands related to these prophecies:

Psalm 96:3, "Declare his glory among the nations (*goyim*), his marvelous deeds among all peoples."

Jeremiah 31:10, "Hear the word of the LORD, you nations (*goyim*); proclaim it in distant coastlands."

The Great Multitude

Finally, in Revelation 7:9-10, we are given a beautiful picture of the fulfillment of these prophecies.

> After this I looked, and there before me was a great multitude that no one could count, from every nation, tribe, people and language, standing before the throne and before the Lamb. They were wearing white robes and were holding palm branches in their hands. And they cried out in a loud voice: "Salvation belongs to our God, who sits on the throne, and to the Lamb."

I can't wait for that day! What an awesome worship service that will be!

Do you know what I find interesting about this? Not only was it prophesied that one day God will be exalted in all nations, but it was commanded that his people help make that happen. In other words, we are commanded to help fulfill a prophecy.

How cool is that?! God promised that one day all nations would hear. And at the same time, he is commanding us to go help make that happen. That's the kind of assignment I like.

So how are we doing right now?

Researchers believe that today (as of this writing), there are about 17,014 people groups or ethnos in the world, diversified by language AND culture.[1] Going back to our orchard, the 17,000 apple trees represent those 17,014 people groups.

What is truly amazing is that, in today's world, with advanced communications, a global community, and large numbers of people going on missions, it is believed that, as of this writing, there are **7,063 ethnos, or people groups, who would be considered unevangelized.**[2]

An unevangelized people group is made up of people of whom the majority have never heard the gospel with such cultural and personal relevance that it results in their sufficient understanding to accept or reject Jesus Christ by faith.

It can be hard for us to comprehend that there are still people who know very little, or nothing at all, about Jesus. But there are a lot of them. Let me share a story about one of these people, whom I met several years ago.

A Personal Encounter

In 1998, I was on a summer missions project in a closed, Muslim country. It was illegal for us to share the gospel there, so we had to be careful, but through taking classes on a local university campus, we were able to meet a number of residents. One of the people I met just outside the university was a street vendor named Diad. He told me that he had been a soldier in the Iraqi army during the first Gulf War, and was in this country

---

1   Joshua Project. 2018. "Global Statistics." People Groups. Accessed Accessed Feb 25, 2019 https://joshuaproject.net/
2   Ibid

temporarily to try to earn some money and enjoy some relative peace.

One night, my wife and I saw Diad as we were walking home from dinner, and so I introduced her to him. She asked, "Where are you from?"

At this, Diad hung his head and said, "I am your enemy."

I replied quickly, "No, Diad, we are followers of Jesus and we have no enemies. We may not like everything your government has done, but we love the Iraqi people."

His face suddenly brightened. "I love the Jesus! The Jesus is wonderful!"

So I said, "I'd love to meet with you, and tell you more about 'the' Jesus." We set an appointment the next day to meet at a nearby cafe.

When I met Diad again the next day, he was noticeably nervous.

"Are you okay?" I asked.

"In Iraq," he said, "if we even talk to a foreigner, we can be tortured." I hadn't realized the risk he was willing to take to learn more about Jesus, but I was grateful, and tried to reassure him.

"We should be safe in this country, but we can talk quietly, so as not to arouse suspicion."

I began to explain the gospel simply and clearly to him by using a gospel tool that was in both English and Arabic. A few minutes into our conversation, a police car pulled up right next to us. Both of us froze, and I saw near panic in Diad's eyes. Fortunately for us, they were just grocery shopping and not interested in us, and we were able to carry on.

As we went through the gospel, Diad was mesmerized. It all made sense to him, so as we came to the prayer, I asked him, "Diad, would you like to invite Jesus to take control of your life?"

His response startled me, as he almost shouted, "*Everything*

I know about Jesus is what you have told me these last 30 minutes! How can I make a decision like that?"

"I totally understand. Let's meet again tomorrow in a safer location, and we can talk some more," I suggested.

The next day, we decided to meet in my apartment, joined by a couple of friends of mine. Diad asked that we enter the home separately, so as not to arouse suspicion. After getting us all inside, I closed the curtains, and we started answering some of Diad's questions. The other guys shared their testimonies, and we shared some more promises of God. At one point, I asked again, "Diad, would you like to invite Jesus to take control of your life?"

Again, he exclaimed, "*Everything* I know about Jesus is what you have told me these past two days. How can I make that decision?"

"I completely understand," I replied, and we continued to answer questions.

A few minutes later, however, Diad asked a profound question: "If I accept Jesus, do I need to tell anybody?"

"Initially, no." I responded, "We will connect you with some Christians who can help you grow in your faith. But eventually, you will need to take a stand for Jesus." Diad nodded his head, and we continued our discussion.

Several minutes later, Diad surprised us all.

"I am ready," he said. "I am ready to receive the Jesus."

"Are you sure?" I said, "We don't want to rush you." Diad nodded his head, and we led him through the prayer to give Jesus control of his life.

I wanted him to understand that his salvation was based on faith, accepting God's free gift, and not on works. So I asked him a question. "Diad, if you were to die tonight, how certain would you be that you would go to heaven?"

He shook his head sadly, and said, "I am a very bad man. Fifty percent!"

We then showed him Scriptures that confirmed that his salvation had nothing to do with his performance, but depended entirely on his receiving God's free gift of Jesus by faith. His countenance began to brighten as this truth sunk in. So I asked him again about his certainty of going to heaven.

This time, he exclaimed, "One hundred percent! Why won't you let me tell anybody about this?!"

We laughed and explained that we would love for him to tell others, but he would have to be careful. Over the next few days, Diad did begin to share the gospel with his friends, compelled by the incredible news that he had just learned.

I share this story because, while it is so encouraging to see Diad's response to the gospel the first time he heard it, there are literally **billions** of people like Diad who have never had the chance to hear even once about Jesus' love and plan for them.

Billions of Unreached Peoples

There are many great online resources to help us understand the Church's progress in taking the gospel to all nations. I have found joshuaproject.net particularly helpful, as it provides statistics on every known people group in the world. On this website, they define Christian adherents as "anyone who professes to be Christian. The term embraces all traditions and confessions of Christianity. It is no indicator of the degree of commitment or theological orthodoxy."

They define "evangelicals" as "followers of Christ who generally emphasize: 1) The Lord Jesus Christ as the sole source of salvation through faith in Him. 2) Personal faith and conversion with regeneration by the Holy Spirit. 3) A recognition of the inspired Word of God as the only basis for faith and living. 4) Commitment to Biblical preaching and evangelism that brings others to faith in Christ."[3] With these definitions in mind, let me share with you some shocking statistics from the Joshua Project website about a few of the least reached people groups.

The Jat (Muslim traditions) people group of Pakistan is made up of 32 million people—about the same size as Canada. The Jat are among the wealthiest people in Pakistan, and have produced a number of political leaders, including a prime minister. Among the Jat in Pakistan, there is an evangelical population of 0.00%. That was surprising, but surely there are many who think of themselves as Christians? In many countries, professing to be a Christian simply means, "I am not a Muslim or Hindu." Among these Jat Muslim people, however, the percentage of professing Christians is also 0.00%.

Next, I learned about the Shaikh people of Bangladesh—population 136 million.

Evangelicals? 0.00%

Professing Christians? 0.00%

How about the Yadav (Hindu traditions) people of India, with a population of 58 million?

Evangelical? 0.00%

Professing Christians? 0.00%

How about the Yemeni people of Northern Yemen, with a population of 11 million?

Evangelicals? 0.00%

Professing Christians? 0.00%

In these least-reached areas, we occasionally encounter some faint hope. For example, among the Turk people in Turkey, population 55 million, we learn that the evangelical population is 0.003%. That works out to about 1650 known believers in a country of 55,000,000 people.

Among the Hui people of China, population 13 million, we see a bit more progress, with an evangelical population of 0.01%,

3   Joshua Project. 2018. Accessed November 29, 2018. https://joshuaproject.net/help/definitions

or about 1 for every 10,000 people. This is progress because just a few years ago, the percentages were both at 0.00%. Praise God! But progress will continue to be slow here because this is a predominantly Sunni Muslim people in China, so it is both illegal and dangerous to share the gospel with them.

These people groups I have listed above are just a few of the 7,063 unreached people groups in our world as of this writing. Those people groups represent about 3.1 *billion* people. And every day, about 50,000 of these people die without ever hearing about the good news of Jesus. This is tragic!

What About The Needs In North America?

Whenever I share these stats and stories, I inevitably encounter people who point out that there are significant needs in North America. I agree! But according to Joshua Project, in the US, the evangelical population is 26.4%, and Christian adherents make up 77.3%.[4] In Canada, the numbers are a little lower, with evangelicals totalling 8% and Christian adherents making up 73.5%.[5] What a contrast to these unreached people groups we just looked at! We must continue to take the gospel to the people in North America. But we cannot ignore the massive need of taking the gospel to the least-reached peoples.

Some have argued that if we send everyone to the least reached, there will be no one left for North America. But if you look at where the Christian workers are now, you will see that this is not a concern at this point. According to The Travelling Team's website, there are approximately 5.5 million Christian workers in the world—pastors, missionaries, and other full-time Christian workers. Of these, only 20,500, or about 0.37%, are

---

4   Joshua Project. 2018. "United States". People Groups. Accessed November 29, 2018. https://joshuaproject.net/countries/US
5   Joshua Project. 2018. "Canada". People Groups. Accessed November 29, 2018. https://joshuaproject.net/countries/CA

working among the 3.1 billion unreached peoples of the world.[6] It appears that there is little danger of the North American church "over-sending" to the least reached any time soon.

Going back to my orchard analogy, the state of the Great Commission is a lot like that of the orchard. There are lots of people working, but most of the work is happening in places where there are already other workers. That is typical because we respond to what we can see. The needs of North America tend to move us because they are right in front of us. It's a little tougher to see the needs in the slums of India or remote villages of the Middle East and Africa.

One of my favourite passages is Romans 15:20-22, where the Apostle Paul shares his passion:

> It has always been my ambition to preach the gospel where Christ was not known, so that I would not be building on someone else's foundation. Rather, as it is written: "Those who were not told about him will see, and those who have not heard will understand." This is why I have often been hindered from coming to you.

Paul often passed up ministering to those who had already heard, because his passion was to proclaim the gospel to those who had not yet heard. In the orchard analogy, unpicked fruit dying on the ground is sad. But in the real world, there are millions of real people who will die without ever having had an opportunity to hear about our Lord and Savior, Jesus Christ.

This is tragic.

This is unacceptable.

This should make us weep.

So what can we do about this? I'd like to suggest four practical steps: pray, give, send and go. Let's look at each of these.

---

6   TheTravelingteam. 2018. http://www.thetravelingteam.org/stats/. Accessed November 29, 2018

Let's Get Practical

Pray

The most obvious starting point is to pray for the world. Let me suggest that you make a list of nations or people groups that you would like to see impacted with the gospel, and then begin praying for them. As you read news reports from around the world, begin to pray that God will open hearts among those people, and draw people to himself. Ask God to allow your church or campus ministry to be involved in reaching those people groups with the gospel.

There are great prayer resources such as Operation World or Caleb Project or Joshua Project. Use these to find up-to-date information to help you pray more specifically and intelligently.

During the 1980s, there were a number of people concerned about Eastern Europe, which had been closed off to the gospel because of communism. So prayer movements were launched to specifically pray that God would open doors for the gospel in these closed nations. Over the next several years, communism fell in Eastern Europe, and there was a great spiritual harvest in places like the former Soviet Union, Romania, Yugoslavia and others.

Similarly, in the early 1990s, there seemed to be a number of groups that adopted China in prayer. Then, throughout the late '90s and early 2000s, there was an incredible movement of God that transformed the nation. To illustrate that growth, consider that in 1980, it was estimated that there were about 1 million Christians in China. Today, that number has exploded to over 100 million.[7] And in an exciting development, the church in China has begun sending missionaries to other nations as well, particularly other closed nations in their region.

---

7   Joshua Project. 2018. "China. People Groups. Accessed November 29, 2018. https://joshuaproject.
net/countries/CH

Prayer movements for the Muslim world picked up steam in the late 1990s. Since that time, millions of Muslims have come to faith, with many pointing to dreams and visions of Jesus as the key to their conversion.[8] Let's continue to ask God to work supernaturally in difficult places - even where there are no missionaries!

Related to that, let's pray for laborers for these places. Remember that in Matthew 9:37-38, Jesus commanded us to beg the Lord of the harvest to raise up laborers for the harvest. Pray that God raises up laborers from your church or campus or local ministry to take the gospel to the nations.

Give

The amount of money being given to reach the least-reached peoples with the gospel is staggeringly small. According to The Travelling Team website, it is estimated that globally, the annual income of evangelical Christians is about $7 trillion per year. Of this, we give about $45 billion or **0.6%** to missions. And how much do we give to the least reached peoples? About $450 million, or **0.006%**.[9] No wonder progress is so slow in these areas!

It can be difficult to know how to give to the least reached, but with a little bit of research and intentionality, we can focus our giving towards these areas. My wife and I often know of students or church people going on missions trips. We obviously can't give to them all, so we prioritize those taking the gospel to the Muslim world or other closed nations. Perhaps you could seek out missions agencies that focus on the least-reached, such as Frontiers or Pioneers, and find ways of supporting their work.

8   Academia. 2015. "Believers in Christ from a Muslim Background: A Global Census."
    Interdisciplinary Journal of Research and Religion. Article 10.Vol 11. Accessed November 30, 2018.
    https://www.academia.edu/16338087/Believers_in_Christ_from_a_Muslim_Background_A_
    Global_Census
9   Travelling Team. 2018. http://www.thetravelingteam.org/stats/ Accessed November 29, 2018

Also, many of us sponsor children through groups like
World Vision or Compassion. When selecting your child, why
not prioritize children who live in nations that are traditionally
closed to the gospel?

Finally, consider investing in nationals who are ministering
in least-reached areas. You can reach out to international organizations such as Cru (Power to Change in Canada) or Navigators
or InterVarsity and ask to support their national staff workers
in closed nations. These organizations should be able to connect
you with their staff in these places, and you could interview
them to decide if you would like to invest in their ministry.

Send

Ralph Winter, who led the US Center for World Missions,
and who was one of the leaders in educating the Church
about the Great Commission, said, "Anyone who can help 100
missionaries to the field is more important than one missionary
on the field."

So, how many missionaries do you want to see raised up or
mobilized from your campus or your church or your ministry?
Sometimes it is as simple as asking the question, "Have you ever
prayerfully considered taking part in a short-term missions trip?"

Go

I find it funny how people respond to considering a missions
trip vs. just about any other trip. Let me give you two scenarios:

Scenario A
>   Bob: "Hey, some buddies and I are going to Mexico over
>   spring break! Do you want to go?"
>   Josh: "Let's do it! Woo Hoo!"

Scenario B

> Bob: "Hey, some of us are going to take the gospel to Mexico over spring break! Do you want to go?"
> Josh: "Let me pray about it."

Obviously, we need to pray about things like this, but Jesus very clearly said, "Go make disciples of all nations." So, in light of that, I believe that every believer can plan on taking part in one short-term missions trip during their lifetime. Obviously, if you are looking at making a long-term move, you need to seek a lot of counsel and spend a lot of time in prayer. However, every believer can, in faith, plan on spending one week on a short-term missions trip. With today's ease of travel, you can hop on a plane, engage with believers in other cultures, get a first-hand perspective on the needs of the world, and be back just a few days later.

It is one thing to read statistics and hear stories. It is another thing entirely to experience the openness to the gospel in Latin American countries, or to meet someone in a closed nation who has never heard anything about Jesus. It will change your life. And it may change the eternal destiny of those you meet.

The Apostle Paul makes it so simple in Romans 10:13-15:

> "Everyone who calls on the name of the Lord will be saved." How, then, can they call on the one they have not believed in? And how can they believe in the one of whom they have not heard? And how can they hear without someone preaching to them? And how can they preach unless they are sent? As it is written, "How beautiful are the feet of those who bring good news!"

We need more beautiful feet bringing good news to the nations!

If you are in university, the time to go is now. When you graduate, your boss will not say to you, "Why don't you take a week off, or even seven weeks, to go on a missions trip?" If you are in the workplace, invest one week's holidays in taking the gospel to another nation. No matter what stage of life you are in, let me strongly encourage you to plan on taking at least one short-term missions trip in the next three years. If you don't build it into your schedule, it likely won't happen.

If possible, in light of the needs of the Great Commission that we just discussed, prioritize taking the gospel to least reached nations. Listen to Paul's heart in Romans 15:20-22:

> It has always been my ambition to preach the gospel where Christ was not known, so that I would not be building on someone else's foundation. Rather, as it is written: "Those who were not told about him will see, and those who have not heard will understand." This is why I have often been hindered from coming to you.

Paul prioritized the unreached people because others would not. I have always been inspired by a quote I heard when I was in university. "Do not give yourselves to that which others can or will do, but to that which others cannot or will not do."

Regardless of the location, let me encourage you to invest just one week during your lifetime to taking the greatest news in history to people in another nation. God will use it to expand your vision and better understand his heart for the world.

One Final Thought

I want to conclude this chapter with one final thought:

The Great Commission will be fulfilled. One day, God will be exalted in every nation. There are only two variables:

1. How soon will it happen?
2. What role will **you** play in seeing it happen?

I pray that you allow God to use you to be a part of his master plan to draw people from every nation, tribe, people and tongue to himself. We will have an eternity to celebrate.

CHAPTER 9

Tying It All Together

I started off this book talking about how, as an 18 year old, I had dreamed that God would allow me to have an impact on the world for Jesus. But during a trip to Haiti, my dream collided with the harsh reality of an immense world with overwhelming needs and challenges.

Today, I have come full circle. I am still asking God to allow me to impact the world for the gospel . . . and I have seen God use me in greater ways than I could have ever dreamed.

As I said at the beginning of this book, following all of these principles is not a guarantee of ministry "success." And I don't pretend to know the plans God has for your life. God can never be put into a box, nor can ministry success be put into a tidy "formula."

Plus, it is important to recognize that ministry fruit does not come overnight. The stories I have shared in this book have occurred over 30 years of full-time ministry, and there have been long stretches when I didn't see amazing things happen. But as we remain faithful, I believe God will bless our efforts.

Importance of God's Word

I also want to emphasize that, in order to have a God-honoring, God-sized vision, we will need to know and apply God's Word. God went to the trouble of providing us with his Word to allow us to know him, understand his will, and enjoy a life that is pleasing to him. So we should read it, study it, memorize it and apply it to our lives.

I believe that God's Word is clear on God's call for believers

to impact the world around them. And I believe, in alignment
with God's Word, that we can move ahead in faith with biblical-
ly-centered plans to have a broad Kingdom impact for his glory.

In II Peter 3:9, it says that the Lord is "not wanting anyone
to perish, but that everyone to come to repentance." And in
John 15:8, Jesus says, "This is to my Father's glory, that you bear
much fruit, showing yourselves to be my disciples." And, of
course, in the Great Commission, Jesus commanded that all of
his disciples make disciples of **all** nations. I believe that these
passages and many others point to God's desire for his Church—
which includes you and me—to have a far-reaching impact for
his Kingdom and his glory. I am not talking about fame and
fortune—this is not about expanding *my* kingdom. This is about
expanding God's Kingdom and allowing Jesus to change lives all
over the world for *his* glory.

I believe that if you apply any one of the principles that I
have laid out in this book, God will allow you to have a significant impact for his Kingdom. But if you apply several, or all, of
these principles as a way of life, you will be amazed at the scope
of impact that God will allow you to see.

I would like to spend the remainder of this book reviewing
these principles, and giving you an opportunity to develop
specific action plans for each one of them.

What are You Trusting God For? Start with a God-sized Vision

The God we see described in Scripture is awesome and supernaturally powerful. I believe that our vision should flow out of
that fact. He created the universe with a word, parted the Red
Sea, and provided both manna from heaven and water from a
rock for the wandering Israelites. He brought down fire from
heaven, and then stopped and started rain in accordance with
Elijah's prayers. He wove together history to align Jesus' birth
with prophecies issued several hundred years before. And just

when Satan thought he had won a great victory by seeing Jesus
on the cross, God demonstrated his sovereign power by raising
Jesus from the dead. If God can do all of these things, then you
and I can trust him for big things.

You may remember that in my first year at Baylor, some
friends and I started dreaming about how God could use
our campus to impact the world. After reading a book called
Fireseeds of Spiritual Awakening, by Dan Hayes, I was inspired by
stories of God's supernatural impact on university campuses. "If
God used those people to do big things," I reasoned, "why can't
he use me?"

So, in my first year in university, I prayed that God would,
in accordance with Matthew 9:37-38 (beg the Lord of the harvest
for laborers), use Baylor to become an amazing sending ground
of Christian workers helping to fulfill the Great Commission.
Years later, I am still amazed at how God continues to answer
those prayers by using many of my peers and other Baylor
alumni to impact the world with the gospel.

When I moved out to Ontario to oversee the campus ministry, my first act as a regional director was to print t-shirts that
said, "We are here to change the world!" As I met with staff and
students, I would often say to them, "Twenty years from now,
wouldn't it be cool if you and I could fly around the world and
meet alumni from our campuses who are impacting the world
for Jesus?!" Over twenty years later, that vision is coming true.
Today, you and I could literally fly around the world and meet
alumni from Ontario campuses who are having a multiplied
impact for our Lord and Savior in multiple nations.

It's been amazing to see other nations pick up this vision as
well. On a missions project in Panama several years ago, while
training our Panamanian leaders, I asked, "What is the vision of
your ministry?"

"We want to impact Panama with the gospel!" they shouted
enthusiastically.

"Too small!" I shouted back. "Over the next four months, India's population will grow by the entire population of Panama. God has commanded the Church to impact the world, and so let's trust God to use your ministry in Panama to impact the world!"

They agreed and embraced that vision.

Over the next several years, the ministry in Panama grew, and they began sending out missionaries from Panama. At first, they sent to the Dominican Republic, and then to Spain, and now they are sending missionaries to the Muslim world. Oliver, the national campus director at the time, has since been asked to give leadership to all of our campus ministries in Latin America, where he is helping them to develop a similar God-sized vision.

So what is your God-sized dream?

Do you want to see millions of Muslims become followers of Jesus?

Do you want to see a radical drop in poverty or in the number of orphans in the world?

Do you want to see the divorce rate in North America drop to single digits?

Do you want to introduce world leaders to Jesus?

Do you want to see the fulfillment of the Great Commission during our lifetime?

Take a few minutes to pray, and then write down a few ideas of what you would like to see God do through you. Make sure that this dream is God-focused, God-glorifying, and aligned with God's will as revealed in his Word.

_____

_____

_____

_____

_____

It is too small a thing for you to be my servant to restore the
tribes of Jacob and bring back those of Israel I have kept. I
will also make you a light for the Gentiles, that my salvation
may reach to the ends of the earth (Isaiah 49:6).

Supernatural Power

A God-honoring, God-sized vision will come, first, from an
understanding of the character and attributes of God as revealed
in the Bible. But to see these dreams become reality, we will
need to develop a lifestyle of prayer and of being filled and
empowered by the Holy Spirit. As these practices permeate every
aspect of your walk with God and ministry, you will ensure that
it is God doing the work, and not just you. And, if it is God
doing the work, we will be more likely to see this vision become
a reality.

When I am filled with the Holy Spirit, I become more God-
focused and less "me-focused." He gives me the desire to impact
others with the gospel, versus just focusing on my own needs
and desires.

When I am filled with the Holy Spirit, I am empowered
to avoid sin, and to allow him to produce fruit in my life that
honors him. When I am not filled with his Spirit, sin can take
over, and I produce fruit that dishonors him. Plus, I am not very
nice to be around.

When I am filled with the Holy Spirit, I am able to overcome my fears related to sharing my faith with others, stepping
out of my comfort zone, or taking on roles and responsibilities
that seem way beyond my abilities.

Simply put, when you and I are filled with the Holy Spirit,
we are more like Jesus. And that is how we can be used by him
to accomplish great things for his glory.

Are there areas of your life that you find difficult to sur-
render to the Lordship of Jesus? Are there sins that you need

to confess? Is there anything that you are holding on to that is blocking the Holy Spirit's power in your life? Ask Jesus to reveal these things to you:

_____

_____

_____

_____

Our Most Dangerous Weapon

With our God-sized vision, a lifestyle of prayer, and being filled with the Holy Spirit, we can confidently pray God-sized prayers.

A few years ago, I decided to start asking God for some huge, seemingly impossible lifetime objectives that were aligned with his will, as revealed in Scripture. My vision was huge, so I figured that I should start offering some massive prayer requests that would allow me to see my vision come true. God is the God of the impossible, and I would love to see these things happen, so why not ask him? I have been amazed at how God has responded to these prayers.

I began asking God to allow me to lead 25 multi-millionaires to Christ. My job allows me to work alongside wealthy, influential leaders, and I know that God "desires none to perish," so I have been praying that God will allow me to introduce these very wealthy people to Jesus. Recently, I have been journeying alongside a very wealthy leader who is just beginning his relationship with Jesus.

I have been praying that God will allow me to impact 1000 world leaders with the gospel. In I Timothy 2:1-2 ESV, Paul urges us to pray for "kings and all who are in high positions, that we may lead a peaceful and quiet life." When I started praying this, I had very little contact with leaders like this, but recently, I have been engaged in a ministry that is focused on ministering to high-ranking government officials in Canada and from around the world. God has given me favor with one high-ranking official from a Muslim country, and we have had several conversations about Jesus.

I have been asking God for many years to allow me to be part of the generation that sees the fulfillment of the Great Commission. As I mentioned earlier, I am now part of a huge foundation whose focus is to fund ministry among the least reached in the world. I am also helping to give leadership to a digital ministry that has several strategies focused on exposing tens of millions of people to the gospel in unreached areas all over the world.

So what are your God-sized prayers? List a few here:

_____

_____

_____

_____

Think Eternally, Live Accordingly

God has entrusted each of us with time, talent and treasure that can be used for anything we choose. If your God-sized vision is focused on impacting eternity, that will compel you to view everything else in light of eternity as well. Think about it:

- Every dollar that I invest in eternal things expands my Kingdom impact.
- Every hour that I invest in eternal things expands my Kingdom impact.
- Every ounce of energy and passion that I pour into eternal things expands my Kingdom impact.

Does this mean that I can't have hobbies, or enjoy entertainment? No! I love sports, going out to dinner, and driving a reliable car. But in light of eternity, and because of my God-sized vision, I prioritize investing my time, talent and treasure in things that will impact the world for Jesus. I try to weigh all of these investments in light of eternity.

I chose to marry Joanne, in large part, because she loves Jesus, and because she possesses an eternal perspective. She also shares my passion to impact the world for Jesus, so our goals are aligned. In light of eternity, when I was single, I only considered dating, and then marrying, a woman who I knew was already a Christian, and who possessed an eternal perspective herself.

My eternal perspective also shaped my career choice. I wanted to give my best hours to having a maximum impact for God's Kingdom, so I chose to pursue full-time Christian ministry. Not everyone is called to this, but eternal perspective allows me to live with the sacrifices that accompany a career in ministry. As I am firmly into mid-life, it is interesting, and sometimes discouraging, to watch the salaries of many of my peers grow exponentially, while mine has grown at a much slower rate. However, my eternal perspective allows me to focus on my "deferred compensation plan," payable in heaven.

For me, many of my decisions are not based on whether they are good or bad, but instead are based on how eternally significant they are.

In light of eternity, what are 2-3 action steps you can take with regard to your time, talent and treasures to have a maximum Kingdom impact?

_____

_____

_____

_____

Change the Trees

When God changes hearts, the fruit follows. Sometimes, it happens in rapid bursts, such as during the revival in Wales described in chapter 5. But most of the time, it happens over a longer period of time, as new believers grow and mature.

I remember being very emotional at Erik's wedding. When I first met Erik, he was sleeping with his girlfriend, and living a life mostly for himself. I had helped introduce Erik to faith several years before that day, and had then invested the next 3 years discipling him. After coming to faith, Erik broke up with that girlfriend, began to grow in his faith, and developed a passion to impact others for Christ. Over the next several years, Erik introduced others to faith, inspired students to go on missions, and ended up spending a couple of years in a least reached country, leading Muslims to Christ. Upon his return, he continued to make disciples at a midwestern university, where he met his future wife, a godly woman who had a heart to impact the world, and together, they continued to have a multiplied impact. Everywhere Erik went, God was using him to change the trees.

At his wedding, I saw the large number of people Erik had impacted for the Kingdom. When I introduced myself to his mother, her eyes flew open and she exclaimed, "Gregg! You changed our family!" You see, after I trained Erik to share his faith, he went home and led both his mother and sister to Christ, as well as a few of his friends. His sister, who later married a Christian man, was at the wedding with their young child, who was going to have the privilege of growing up in a Christian home.

A few years later, Erik developed a brain tumour, and died at the age of 35. During his illness, he received messages of support from friends and acquaintances from over 20 nations. A bad tree was changed into a good tree, which then was involved in changing trees all over the world. We won't know the ramifications of those changes until eternity, but they will be massive. We've seen these changes time and again:

- John Newton, the wicked slave trader, is transformed into a Christ-centered hymn writer who wrote "Amazing Grace."
- Charles Colson, driven and conniving "hatchet man" for US former President Richard Nixon, is transformed into the founder and leader of Prison Fellowship, which has introduced millions of inmates to Jesus.
- Bub Millard, the abusive father of Bart Millard (lead singer of Mercy Me, and writer of "I Can Only Imagine") is transformed from a brutal monster into a loving, gentle follower of Jesus.
- Muslim jihadists give up their commitment to terrorism following encounters with Jesus.

As we focus on changing the trees, individual hearts are transformed, and the Holy Spirit produces fruit that transforms families, communities and nations.

List the names of friends and acquaintances, or even people groups, whom you would like to see transformed by the gospel over the next few years. If you are able, consider making a plan to reach out to these people and share the gospel with them.

_____

_____

_____

_____

Ever-expanding Faith

I have learned that if I want to see God do big things through me, my faith needs to be stretched far beyond where it is now.

And in order for my faith to grow, I need to develop a habit of intentionally expanding my faith.

One recent example of this came about a year ago, when I decided to get out of my comfort zone and try to meet the Chief of Police in my hometown, and see if I could initiate a spiritual conversation with him.

On the day I scheduled to do this (I put it in my calendar), I was really nervous. In fact, I was almost shaking when I approached the desk of an unfriendly looking officer in the police station and asked if I could speak to the Chief of Police.

"Why do you want to speak to him?" he asked.

Nervously, I replied, "I work near here, and I am part of a local church, and I wanted to get his perspective and insights into some different issues in the community."

Warily, he left to find the Chief. When the head of police came out, I explained my intentions, and set up an appointment to meet with him. A couple of days later, I went in with a small, informal survey. Again, I was nearly shaking with fear as I went to meet him. But I found him to be gracious and open to talk. In fact, he was quite excited to hear about the ways our church could potentially help impact the community.

While I did not get a chance to share the gospel that day, I was able to invite him to an outreach event a few weeks later. Unfortunately, he was not able to attend, and shortly after, moved to another division. But I had grown in my faith that day, and I had overcome my fear with a Spirit-filled boldness that allowed me to see the goodness of God at work.

Remember the multi-millionaire I have been helping in his spiritual journey? In the weeks leading up to our meeting, I prayed that God would give me the boldness to share with him, and the opportunity to bring up the topic. We had talked about God before, but I rehearsed in my mind a few ways that I could initiate a spiritual conversation about where his spiritual life was ("May I ask you a personal question? I'd love to get an idea of where you stand regarding your relationship with God."). Then, right in his office, I asked him a few of those questions, and took the opportunity to share the gospel. God used that step of faith to allow me to help a very influential leader get his life right with God.

What step of faith could you take to grow your faith in the next 2-3 months?

_____

_____

_____

_____

The Power of Multiplication

In my opinion, spiritual multiplication is the most powerful ministry strategy that Jesus provided us with. Applying this principle alone will allow you to expand your Kingdom impact 100-fold. This is why one of my life quotes is from John Mott, who said, as I shared in chapter 7, "He who does the work is not so profitably employed as he who multiplies the doers." The more you can apply this principle, the broader your Kingdom impact will be.

Over the past few weeks, I have been able to have conversations with several young men whom I inspired when they were in college. I think of Ted and Chris, who together planted a church about eight years ago, which has grown to over 800 people. They have already planted a second church, and are in the process of planting another (spiritual multiplication for churches!)

Arvind was heading to a career in engineering, but God used our time together to inspire him to pursue a life of ministry. Today, he pastors a church of over 500 members in Northern

India. A few years ago, Arvind introduced a man to faith who now has a heart for the Dalits or "untouchables" in India. Over the past few years, this man has introduced over 100 Dalits to faith, and recently planted a church with 150 people in it. How is that for multiplication?! I have never visited India, but through Arvind, I am having an impact.

My favorite part about spiritual multiplication is that we won't know the extent of the impact until we get to heaven. People we influence for Jesus go on to influence many others, and there is no way of keeping track (though Jesus is doing that!). But if you equip the people you are discipling with a vision and tools to multiply, you can be guaranteed that your influence will continue to multiply for years to come.

Through multiplication, my Kingdom reach can extend to people in multiple countries and in multiple languages. I simply focus on making disciples who make disciples.

List 1-2 ways you can multiply yourself over the next 12 months

_____

_____

_____

_____

Exalted in Every Nation

How many nations does your God-sized vision include? Jesus' God-sized vision for his disciples was that they would multiply to impact the world. Every additional nation in which we invest our time, talent or treasures expands our Kingdom impact. I am constantly looking for ways to expand the reach of the gospel. Here are a few ideas for you to ensure a global impact.

1. When you lead a prayer group, focus on fulfilling the Great Commission
2. When you make disciples, focus on fulfilling the Great Commission
3. When you invest your money, prioritize fulfilling the Great Commission.
4. When you develop your personal life plan and goals, focus on fulfilling the Great Commission.

List 3-4 action steps you can take to help advance the fulfillment of the Great Commission:

_____

_____

_____

_____

One Additional Component - Perseverance

Before we wrap up, I want to emphasize one last key to seeing God use you to have a maximum Kingdom impact: Don't give up.

I remember being completely exhausted during my second year in Ontario. I had been working incredibly hard in ministry, but I didn't feel like we were making much progress. The stresses of ministry were making me consider giving up altogether and quitting. Then I came across this passage in Galatians 6:9 NASB: "Let us not lose heart in doing good, for in due time we will reap if we do not grow weary."

I was gripped by the phrase, "in due time." The Apostle Paul was saying that as I remained faithful in doing good, in due time, I would reap the fruit of my labors. I was trusting God for big things, but I also needed to trust God for his timing.

There have been multiple times in my ministry career that I

have wanted to quit. The stresses of ministry would overwhelm
me, and I would start looking in the classified ads jobs postings.
But by the Holy Spirit, God allowed me to keep going and
continue to expand my impact.

If I had quit after my first year of ministry, I would never
have seen Erik turn into a multiplying missionary.

If I had quit after my eighth year in ministry, I would never
have seen Diad come to faith.

If I had quit after my ninth year in ministry, I would never
have seen thousands of students go on short-term or long-term
missions through our ministry.

If I had quit after my 25th year in ministry, I would have
never seen God provide a $100 million gift towards fulfilling the
Great Commission.

I believe God blesses perseverance, and as we remain faithful,
in due time, he will reward us.

Final Thoughts

God wants to use us to advance his Kingdom. He has laid out
clear principles in Scripture to help us do just that. The great
news is that we don't have to be brilliant or exceptionally gifted.
All he asks for is our availability and obedience, allowing him to
work in and through us.

My prayer for you is that you will allow God to use you
in supernatural ways, bringing great glory to him, all over the
world. I am praying that he will use you to rapidly advance Jesus'
Great Commission. And I am praying that God will allow us to
be a part of changing the world for his glory!

Acknowledgements

Thank you, Joanne, for being my wife and for being my biggest cheerleader and encourager. You patiently endured my working on this book through weekends and holidays, and encouraging me through the many times I wanted to give up. I am so grateful for your love for me and for your passion to impact the world for Jesus.

Thank you, Keisha Johnson, for your great wisdom, patience and encouragement throughout the editing process. I am so grateful for your expert guidance through this project, and for your gentle prodding when I was ready to give up.

Thank you, Laurie Armstrong, for proofreading my book, and offering many excellent insights. You have been a faithful friend for many years.

Thank you Andrew Alexander, Andrew Tai, Archie Kenyon, Arvind Balaram, Byron Chae, Chris Shipley, David Au Yeung, Ethan Park, Alex Philip, Jeanette Ravoka, Jeremy Carroll, Kevin Cuz, Kirk Durston, Mark Peterson, Mark Josephs, Mike Woodard, Oliver Marin, Paul Henderson, Rick Reed, Steve Martin, Steve Strongitharm, Tariku Fufa, Ted Duncan and Uche Anizor. You each took time to read my manuscript at various stages of development, and provided feedback to allow me to sharpen and refine the final product. Thank you!!!

Thank you, Miller Alloway, Rick Franklin, Sharon Simmonds, and other leaders at Arrow Leadership for the strong encouragement to write this book, and for affirming and strengthening my identity in Christ.

Thank you Heather Bell, for serving as my executive assistant through much of this process, ensuring that I had the time and capacity to complete this work. You have been a huge blessing to my life and ministry!

Thank you to my many ministry partners who have invested prayers and resources in my family and me over these past 30 years. Together, we have seen God work in and through this ministry. We are so grateful for you!

Thank you, Cheryl Cardon, for helping me think through compelling ways to communicate my ideas to a broader audience.

Thank you, Bill Livingstone, for providing the illustrations for this book.

Thank you, Bill Glasgow, for your help with my cover design and for preparing my manuscript for publishing.

Thank you, Josh and Jessica, for your encouragement in writing this book, and Jessica for the back cover photograph. I love you both!